TABLE OF CONTENTS

GENERAL INFORMATION

(INTENTIONALLY BLANK)

United States Joint Forces Command (USJFCOM) Joint Warfighting Center (JWFC) MISSION: To support joint and multi-national training and exercises focused on commanders, staffs, and component forces; assisting the Chairman of the Joint Chiefs of Staff (CJCS), and Service Chiefs in their preparation for joint and combined operations in their preparation for joint and combined operations; and to facilitate the conceptualization, development, and assessment of joint doctrine.

OVERVIEW: The JWFC is a USJFCOM organization designed to support all training and exercise programs throughout the joint training cycle. The USJFCOM JWFC also supports joint doctrine development and assessment, both for current needs and future concepts for joint operations. The USJFCOM JWFC is an on-line organization experienced in exercise support and doctrine development. The USJFCOM JWFC currently is developing joint training functions and capabilities.

JOINT COURSE AND COURSEWARE CATALOG DESCRIPTION: The Joint Course and Courseware Catalog (JCCC) is a reference of available joint training courses and joint training courseware that address aspects of joint and multinational operations. The primary purpose is to provide access to joint course information from a single, comprehensive source. The Services and their components, formal schools, individual CINC Staffs and other training sponsors and activities, provided inputs. All the courses submitted are included and the information listed for each course is as provided by the sponsoring activity. The JCCC is available in hard copy, on-line with the Joint Electronic Library (JEL), or as a formatted CD-ROM with the JEL. To obtain JEL access or to request a CD-ROM; write to the Commander, USJFCOM/J7, Joint Warfighting Center, Attn: Joint Doctrine Division, 116 Lakeview Parkway, Suffolk, VA 23435-2697; Telephone Commercial (757) 686-6113/61114; DSN 668; Commercial FAX (757) 686-6199. It is available on the USJFCOM JWFC Homepage at: http:/www-secure.jwfc.jfcom.mil/protected/doctrine/jcc99/online/

INSTRUCTIONS FOR USING THE JCCC: The catalog is organized to facilitate ready reference to courses and to provide general course information and administrative instructions. Courses are listed according to levels of war as defined by the Universal Joint Task List (UJTL), Version 4.0, CJCSM 3500.04B, 1 October 1999 (see Figure 2-1 on page 2-5):

- Strategic National Military Level (SN)
- Strategic Theater Level (ST)
- Operational Level (OP)
- Tactical Level (TA)

Courses are grouped numerically by UJTL Reference, and listed alphabetically by title in the following format:

Title:
UJTL Reference:
Course Number:
Objective:
Description:
Audience:
Clearance:
Prerequisites:
Length:
Frequency:
Capacity:
Location:
VTC:
Location:
Distance Learning:
Cost:
Funding:
Curriculum Manager:
CMDSN:
CMCOMM:
CMDSNFAX:
CMCOMMFAX:
CMCOMME-MAIL:
Scheduling Activity:
SADSN:
SADSNFAX:
SACOMME-MAIL:
Reviewing Activity:

The UJTL Reference reflects the focus of the course but does not necessarily limit attendance to those serving in that particular position or on a staff at that level. The UJTL is a guide to be used in conjunction with the course objective, description, audience, clearance and prerequisites for determining the attendance criteria. Administrative information regarding length, frequency, cost, funding, curriculum manager, and scheduling activity is provided to assist you in coordinating attendance.

INSTRUCTIONS FOR RECOMMENDATIONS AND INPUTS: Preparation of the JCCC is the responsibility of the USJFCOM J7/Commander, USJFCOM Joint Warfighting Center. Users are invited to send comments and suggestions as indicated in Appendix A. The USJFCOM JWFC also welcomes recommendations for additional courses to be included in catalog updates. Submission of course data should be provided as indicated in Appendix B. The information provided should be forwarded directly to the address listed below.

> USJFCOM Joint Warfighting Center
> ATTN: Joint Doctrine Division
> 116 Lakeview Parkway
> Suffolk, VA 23435-2697

Telephone: Commercial (757) 686-6113/6114; DSN 668-6113; FAX 686-6199

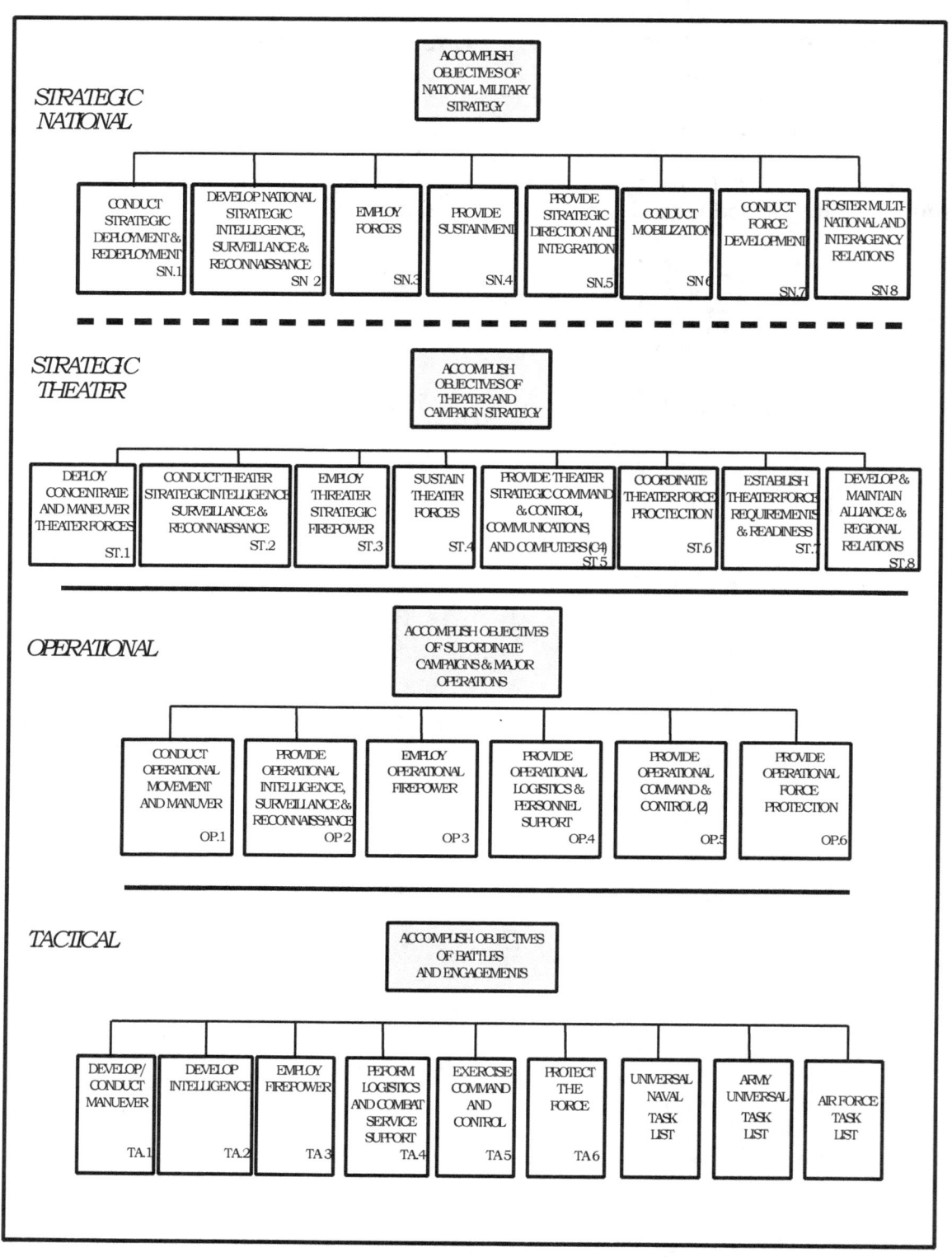

UNIVERSAL JOINT TASK LIST (UJTL)
(Figure 1)

Title:	**ADVERSARIAL DECEPTION AWARENESS COURSE (ADAC)**
UJTL Reference:	SN.2, SN.3
Course Number:	N/A
Objective:	To know the threat of Deception and denial to systems and assets. Introduces students to the historical, psychological, cultural, technological and operational aspects of hostile Deception. While the course has some concentration on former Soviet issues, it is designed to include significant issues facing national decision-makers and a wide range of analytical, functional, and geographic areas (e.g., arms control, counterdrug, third world activities, etc.).
Description:	Sessions are presented using various methods of instruction, including lectures by experts from DIA, CIA, NSA, other government agencies, and contract personnel, videos, and case studies.
Audience:	Any intelligence analyst.
Clearance:	TOP SECRET/SCI/TK/G
Prerequisites:	NONE
Length:	4 days
Frequency:	3 classes per year
Capacity:	Varies
Location:	JMITC, Bolling AFB, MD
VTC:	NONE
Distance Learning:	NONE
Cost:	Per Diem and travel to the training location.
Funding:	By parent organization
Curriculum Manager:	JMITC, DAJ-1
CMDSN:	428-2791
CMCOMM:	(202) 231-2791
CMDSNFAX:	428-8497
CMCOMMFAX:	(202) 373-8497
CMCOMME-Mail:	
Scheduling Activity:	JMITC, DAJ-2C
SADSN:	428-3108
SACOMM:	(202) 231-3108
SADSNFAX:	428-2810
SACOMMFAX:	(202) 231-2810
SACOMME-Mail:	
Reviewing Activity:	DIA/JMITC

Title:	**ADVANCED COUNTERTERRORISM ANALYSIS COURSE (ACAC)**
UJTL Reference:	SN.2, SN.3; ST.8
Course Number:	N/A
Objective:	To enhance understanding of the collection and warning processes in the counterterrorism field; to evaluate and discuss intelligence challenges facing terrorism analysts; and to reinforce interaction and coordination among mid-level analysts in the Counterterrorism Community. ACAC is the mid-level course in the JMITC's three-tiered Community Counterterrorism Training Program.
Description:	It emphasizes the pro-active analyst model—the analyst who engages in creative approaches to the terrorism problem and who understands the significant role of collection and warning in dealing with the terrorist threat. ACAC also examines, in detail, important international and domestic terrorism issues. A mixture of hands-on training, speakers, and discussion panels is utilized.
Audience:	Mid-level, O-3/GS-11 or above intelligence analyst status in the Counterterrorism Community. Those of other grades or ranks, with one year or more of counterterrorism analysis may submit a waiver request with their nomination.
Clearance:	TOP SECRET/SCI/TK
Prerequisites:	Applicant must be serving in a counterterrorism analyst position. Attendance in the Counterterrorism Analysis Course (CAC) is recommended but not required. Enrollment is limited to US citizens who are federal government employees.
Length:	1 week
Frequency:	3 classes per year
Capacity:	Varies
Location:	JMITC, Bolling AFB, MD
VTC:	NONE
Distance Learning:	NONE
Cost:	Per diem and travel to the training location.
Funding:	By parent organization
Curriculum Manager:	JMITC, DAJ-1
CMDSN:	428-2791
CMCOMM:	(202) 231-2791
CMDSNFAX:	428-8497
CMCOMMFAX:	(202) 231-8497
CMCOMME-Mail:	
Scheduling Activity:	JMITC, DAJ-2C
SADSN:	428-3108
SACOMM:	(202) 231-3108
SADSNFAX:	428-2810
SACOMMFAX:	(202) 231-2810
SACOMME-Mail:	
Reviewing Activity:	DIA/JMITC

Title:	**COUNTERINTELLIGENCE SPECIAL COURSE (CISC)**
UJTL Reference:	SN.2
Course Number:	N/A
Objective:	To prepare selected DOD and other US government professional counterintelligence officers for sensitive counterintelligence duties involving the International Arms Control Treaties Inspection Program.
Description:	Emphasizing continental United States sites open to foreign inspection under the International Arms Control Treaties Inspection Program, the course covers national CI treaty-related issues: US escort CI debriefing requirements; overviews of treaty protocols, report training; and foreign treaty organizations. Extensive dialogue with dynamic guest speakers.
Audience:	Counterintelligence professionals.
Clearance:	SECRET/NOFORN
Prerequisites:	Attendance is open only to counterintelligence professionals from any US government organization with (treaty inspection) CI responsibilities.
Length:	1 week
Frequency:	2 classes per year
Capacity:	Varies
Location:	JMITC, Bolling AFB, MD
VTC:	NONE
Distance Learning:	NONE
Cost:	Per diem and travel to the training location.
Funding:	By parent organization
Curriculum Manager:	JMITC, DAJ-1C
CMDSN:	428-2791
CMCOMM:	(202) 231-2791
CMDSNFAX:	428-8497
CMCOMMFAX:	(202) 231-8497
CMCOMME-Mail:	
Scheduling Activity:	JMITC, DAJ-2C
SADSN:	428-3108
SACOMM:	(202) 231-3108
SADSNFAX:	428-2810
SACOMMFAX:	(202) 231-2810
SACOMME-Mail:	
Reviewing Activity:	DIA/JMITC; coordinated with OSIA/CI Office

Title:	**COUNTERTERRORISM PERSPECTIVES FOR SENIOR MANAGERS (CTPSM) SEMINAR**
UJTL Reference:	SN.2, SN.3; ST.2; ST.8
Course Number:	N/A
Objective:	To enhance student understanding of counterterrorism and their role in assisting Community coordination and policy formulation; to enable students to develop requirements and direct resources in line with the changing nature of the terrorist threat. This seminar encourages discussion and a free-flow of ideas on a host of terrorist/counterterrorist-related subjects. This interaction not only is an objective in and of itself, but also reinforces the other instructional goals.
Description:	CTPSM is the top-level course in the JMITC's three-tiered Community Counterterrorism Training Program. This is a dynamic seminar which takes into account the changing global environment and the evolving terrorist threat of the 1990's. As a result, the units of instruction/discussion vary depending on the current situation and the needs of the consumers. This adaptability is considered to be one of the most positive characteristics of the seminar. CTPSM focuses on the latest in Community developments, particularly in US CT policy, intelligence, legal, and technological issues.
Audience:	Senior personnel (O-5/GS-14 or above) in counterterrorism management positions. Those of other grades or ranks (not below O-4/E-8/ GS-12) with counterterrorism responsibilities, may apply with a short waiver request included in their nomination.
Clearance:	TOP SECRET/SCI/TK
Prerequisites:	Performs duties related to counterterrorism.
Length:	3 days
Frequency:	3 classes per year
Capacity:	Varies
Location:	JMITC, Bolling AFB, MD
VTC:	NONE
Distance Learning:	NONE
Cost:	Per diem and travel to the training location.
Funding:	By parent organization
Curriculum Manager:	JMITC, DAJ-1
CMDSN:	428-2791
CMCOMM:	(202) 231-2791
CMDSNFAX:	428-8497
CMCOMMFAX:	(202) 231-8497
Scheduling Activity:	JMITC, DAJ-2C
SADSN:	428-3108
SACOMM:	(202) 231-3108
SADSNFAX:	428-2810
SACOMMFAX:	(202) 231-2810
Reviewing Activity:	DIA/JMTC

Title:	**NATIONAL SENIOR INTELLIGENCE COURSE (NSIC)**
UJTL Reference:	SN.2, SN.7
Course Number:	N/A
Objective:	To analyze current national security and future global issues, and developments affecting national level intelligence.
Description:	The course intent is to prepare selected military officers and key civilian personnel for command, staff or policy-making positions in the national and joint intelligence communities. This seminar-style course focuses on global changes affecting the future strategic interests of the US and its allies, and the implications of world change for national, joint, and combined intelligence efforts.
Audience:	Senior-level general intelligence civilian personnel GS-13; military officers 0-4 and above.
Clearance:	TOP SECRET/SCI/TK
Prerequisites:	Duty with national or joint intelligence community.
Length:	2 weeks
Frequency:	3 classes per year
Capacity:	Varies
Location:	JMITC, Bolling AFB, MD
VTC:	NONE
Distance Learning:	NONE
Cost:	Per diem and travel to the training location.
Funding:	By parent organization
Curriculum Manager:	JMITC, DAJ-1
CMDSN:	428-2791
CMCOMM:	(202) 231-2791
CMDSNFAX:	428-8497
CMCOMMFAX:	(202) 231-8497
CMCOMME-Mail:	
Scheduling Activity:	JMITC, DAJ-2C
SADSN:	428-3108
SACOMM:	(202) 231-3108
SADSNFAX:	428-2810
SACOMMFAX:	(202) 231-2810
SACOMME-Mail:	
Reviewing Activity:	DIA/JMITC

Title:	**FEDERAL DRUG ENFORCEMENT INTELLIGENCE SEMINAR (FDEIS)**
UJTL Reference:	SN.2, SN.7, SN.3; ST.8
Course Number:	N/A
Objective:	To orient intelligence personnel with concerns related to counterdrug intelligence collection and production.
Description:	This course for Intelligence Community members directly involved with intelligence support to drug interdiction covers drug identification, law and legal issues applicable to federal drug law enforcement, strategic and operational drug intelligence briefings, conspiracy investigation, smuggling investigation, sources of information, and document analysis. Upon completion, students will have a working knowledge of narcotics and dangerous drugs, an awareness of current drug trafficking trends worldwide, and an understanding of federal drug law enforcement and the mission of the Drug Enforcement Administration.
Audience:	Intelligence personnel dealing with counterdrug intelligence and DEA.
Clearance:	NONE
Prerequisites:	Counterdrug analysts and personnel dealing with the counterdrug problem and interfacing with the DEA.
Length:	8 days
Frequency:	3 classes per year
Capacity:	Varies
Location:	JMITC, Bolling AFB, MD
VTC:	NONE
Distance Learning:	NONE
Cost:	Per diem and travel to the training location.
Funding:	By parent organization
Curriculum Manager:	DEA Training (POC: Ms. Sowers)
CMDSN:	N/A
CMCOMM:	(703) 640-1360
CMDSNFAX:	N/A
CMCOMMFAX:	N/A
CMCOMME-Mail:	
Scheduling Activity:	JMITC, DAJ-2C
SADSN:	428-3108
SACOMM:	(202) 231-3108
SADSNFAX:	428-2810
SACOMMFAX:	(202) 231-2810
SACOMME-Mail:	
Reviewing Activity:	DIA/JMITC

Title:	**COUNTERDRUG INTELLIGENCE ANALYSIS COURSE (CDIAC)**
UJTL Reference:	SN.2; ST.2
Course Number:	N/A
Objective:	To provide a baseline of general and specialized knowledge and competencies in the use of various analytic methodologies applicable to counterdrug intelligence analysis.
Description:	Furnishes analysts with a broad based appreciation of the various elements and issues pertinent to counterdrug intelligence analysis, and exposes the analyst to methodological concepts which assist analytic estimation, assessment and prediction.
Audience:	Any intelligence analyst.
Clearance:	SECRET/NOFORN
Prerequisites:	Students should be assigned, or in transit to, a counterdrug billet or intimately associated with the counterdrug effort.
Length:	1 weeks
Frequency:	2 classes per year
Capacity:	Varies
Location:	JMITC, Bolling AFB, MD
VTC:	NONE
Distance Learning:	NONE
Cost:	Per diem and travel to the training location.
Funding:	By parent organization
Curriculum Manager:	JMITC, DAJ-1
CMDSN:	428-2791
CMCOMM:	(202) 231-2791
CMDSNFAX:	428-8497
CMCOMMFAX:	(202) 231-8497
CMCOMME-Mail:	
Scheduling Activity:	JMITC, DAJ-2C
SADSN:	243-3108
SACOMM:	(202) 231-3108
SADSNFAX:	428-2810
SACOMMFAX:	(202) 231-2810
SACOMME-Mail:	
Reviewing Activity:	DIA/JMITC

Title:	**DEFENSE INTELLIGENCE PRODUCTION ANALYSIS COURSE (DIPAC)**
UJTL Reference:	SN.2
Course Number:	N/A
Objective:	To gain a broad perspective on analysis of foreign defense industries (including proliferation from other countries, arms control, and treaty verification) and an appreciation of the multifaceted activities, accomplishments, vulnerabilities, and weaknesses of foreign defense industrial operations.
Description:	This course is an introduction to the procedures and methodologies used by the Defense Agency for analysis of foreign defense industrial activities and facilities. The skills presented in this course are intended to familiarize analysts responsible for defense industrial studies, proliferation of weapons of mass destruction and advanced conventional weapons, and arms control and treaty verification with the fundamentals of industrial analysis. Through lectures, discussion, practical exercises, and orientation visits to factories, the course provides hands-on experience with industrial analysts. It also describes the type of information required to build estimates of production, bottlenecks and vulnerabilities of factories to work stoppage and interdiction, and potential wartime surge, mobilization, and reconstitution of industrial operations.
Audience:	Mid-level military and civilian personnel (O-3/O-5 and GS-11/13) who are engaged in foreign defense industrial analysis. Nominations must be coordinated through DIA/RAI-2 (Defense Industries Division.)
Clearance:	TOP SECRET/SCI/TK
Prerequisites:	Performs duties in defense industrial analysis.
Length:	2 weeks
Frequency:	2 classes per year
Capacity:	Varies
Location:	JMITC, Bolling AFB, MD
VTC:	Per diem and travel to the training location.
Distance Learning:	NONE
Cost:	NONE
Funding:	By parent organization
Curriculum Manager:	JMITC, DAJ-1
CMDSN:	428-2233
CMCOMM:	(202) 231-3333
CMDSNFAX:	428-8497
CMCOMMFAX:	(202) 231-2753
Scheduling Activity:	JMITC, DAJ-2C
SADSN:	428-2797
SACOMM:	(202) 231-4797
SADSNFAX:	428-2810
SACOMMFAX:	(202) 231-2810
Reviewing Activity:	DIA/JMITC

Title:	**FOREIGN EXCHANGES AND DISCLOSURES COURSE**
UJTL Reference:	SN.2
Course Number:	N/A
Objective:	To provide knowledge of the national policies, rules and regulations that govern exchange agreements and the disclosure of military intelligence to foreign governments and international organizations.
Description:	This is a new course. It has been developed by the Foreign Exchanges and Disclosures Office to meet the need for and the disclosure of military intelligence to foreign governments and international organizations. The course emphasizes the inherent need for foreign disclosure expertise in support of not only coalition operations but support to bilateral relationships as well. The course will provide instruction in determining what military intelligence may or may not be released based on existing policies. Methods taught apply to any intelligence discipline which may be used to support exchange and individual exercises.
Audience:	Anyone who is or will be in a position which requires expertise on the sharing of military intelligence with a foreign government or international organizations. This course is open to all levels of civilian/military personnel. As with any DIA-sponsored training, every consideration will be given to the principles of Equal Employment Opportunity.
Clearance:	TOP SECRET/SI/TK
Prerequisites:	NONE
Length:	5 days
Frequency:	As required
Capacity:	27
Location:	JMITC, Bolling AFB, MD
VTC:	NONE
Distance Learning:	MTT Under Development
Cost:	Unavailable
Funding:	Unavailable
Curriculum Manager:	DIA Joint Military Intelligence Training Center/DAJ-2C
CMDSN:	225-1455
CMCOMM:	(703) 695-1455
CMDSNFAX:	(202) 231-2810
CMCOMMFAX:	428-2810
CMCOMME-Mail:	N/A
Scheduling Activity:	DIA Joint Military Intelligence Training Center/DAJ-2C
SADSN:	428-3108
SACOMM:	(202) 231-3108
SADSNFAX:	428-2810
SACOMMFAX:	(202) 231-2810
SACOMME-Mail:	
Reviewing Activity:	NA

Title:	**INTERSERVICE SPACE INTELLIGENCE OPERATIONS COURSE/MOBILE (ISIOC)**
UJTL Reference:	SN.2; ST.2
Course Number:	V3OZP14N3000
Objective:	Familiarization course for intelligence and space operations officer specialties and civilian equivalents, with newly assigned duties involving space operations that require a basic knowledge of space.
Description:	Course focuses on the joint application of space-related intelligence. The course examines the basic theory and fundamentals of operating in the space environments; space and law policy; military space organizations and missions; US and other countries' space systems and operations; space-related intelligence and collection management; intelligence structure; and the tactical exploitation of national capabilities.
Audience:	O-4 and below and civilian equivalents (O-5 and civilian equivalents may attend).
Clearance:	TOP SECRET/SCI
Prerequisites:	NONE (Personnel with one or more years of space operations and intelligence experience will find this course will not meet their training needs.)
Length:	2 weeks
Frequency:	15 resident classes per year
Capacity:	24 students per class
Location:	Colorado Springs, CO
VTC:	NONE
Distance Learning:	Course V4OST14N3000 is a mobile version of this course; 1 mobile training team per year.
Cost:	Per diem and travel to the training location. Per diem and travel for the mobile training team.
Funding:	By parent organization. By requesting organization for the mobile training team.
Curriculum Manager:	533 TRS (POC: Mr. Ross Wroblewski)
CMDSN:	275-2686
CMCOMM:	(805) 734-2686
CMDSNFAX:	275-0626
CMCOMMFAX:	(805) 734-0626
CMCOMME-Mail:	wroblepr@aetc7204a.vafb.af.mil
Scheduling Activity:	533 TRS
SADSN:	275-2686
SACOMM:	(805) 734-2686
SADSNFAX:	275-0626
SACOMMFAX:	(805) 734-0626
SACOMME-Mail:	wroblepr@aetc7204a.vafb.af.mil
Reviewing Activity:	Community College of the Air Force

Title:	**INTERSERVICE SPACE INTELLIGENCE OPERATIONS SENIOR COURSE**
UJTL Reference:	SN.2; ST.2
Course Number:	V3OZP14N4000
Objective:	Familiarization course for senior intelligence and space operations officers and civilian equivalents, with newly assigned duties involving space operations that require a basic knowledge of space.
Description:	Course focuses on the joint application of space-related intelligence. The course examines the basic theory and fundamentals of operating in the space environment; space law and policy; military space organizations and missions; US and other countries' space systems and operations; space related intelligence and collection management; intelligence structure; and the tactical exploitation of national capabilities.
Audience:	O-5 and above and civilian equivalents.
Clearance:	TOP SECRET/SCI
Prerequisites:	NONE (Personnel with one or more years of space operations and intelligence experience will find this course will not meet their training needs.)
Length:	4 days
Frequency:	4 classes per year
Capacity:	24 students per class
Location:	Colorado Springs, CO
VTC:	NONE
Distance Learning:	NONE
Cost:	Per diem and travel to the training location.
Funding:	By parent organization
Curriculum Manager:	533 TRS (POC: Mr. Ross Wroblewski)
CMDSN:	275-2686
CMCOMM:	(805) 734-2686
CMDSNFAX:	275-0626
CMCOMMFAX:	(805) 734-0626
CMCOMME-Mail:	wroblepr@aetc7204a.vafb.af.mil
Scheduling Activity:	533 TRS
SADSN:	275-2686
SACOMM:	(805) 734-2686
SADSNFAX:	275-0626
SACOMMFAX:	(805) 734-0626
SACOMME-Mail:	wroblepr@aetc7204a.vafb.af.mil
Reviewing Activity:	Community College of the Air Force

Title:	**REGIONAL AREA STUDIES (200 AND 500 SERIES)**
UJTL Reference:	SN.2; ST.2
Course Number:	200 and 500 Series
Objective:	This course highlights the key historical, political, economic, and socio-cultural themes of each world region, conducted at the National Foreign Affairs Training Center (NFATC), Department of State.
Description:	These courses combine lectures, discussions, gaming, and other participatory activities, field trips, and written and audio-visual materials, in order to highlight the key historical, political, economic, and socio-cultural themes of each world region.
Audience:	Policy makers and intelligence personnel.
Clearance:	NONE
Prerequisites:	NONE
Length:	Varies
Frequency:	Varies
Capacity:	Varies
Location:	Arlington, VA
VTC:	NONE
Distance Learning:	NONE
Cost:	Per diem and travel to the training location; $890 tuition.
Funding:	By parent organization
Curriculum Manager:	NFATC/Registrar
CMDSN:	N/A
CMCOMM:	(703) 302-7137
CMDSNFAX:	N/A
CMCOMMFAX:	(703) 302-7152
CMCOMME-Mail:	
Scheduling Activity:	NFATC/Registrar
SADSN:	N/A
SACOMM:	(703) 302-7137
SADSNFAX:	N/A
SACOMMFAX:	(703) 302-7152
SACOMME-Mail:	
Reviewing Activity:	NFATC

Title:	**COUNTERTERRORISM ANALYSIS COURSE (CAC)**
UJTL Reference:	SN.3, SN.2; ST.2, ST.8
Course Number:	N/A
Objective:	To understand major issues confronting counterterrorism analysts, the nature of the terrorist threat, US government organizations and actors involved in US counterterrorism efforts, and the tools and techniques for counterterrorism analysis.
Description:	CAC is the entry-level course in the JMITC's three-tiered Community Counterterrorism Training Program. It introduces analysts to the substance and theory of counterterrorism intelligence analysis, and serves as the baseline for understanding the techniques, tools, procedures supporting timely intelligence on terrorist group behavior, modus operandi, plans, and targets. Requires successful completion of an intensive all-day exercise using the analytical methodologies taught in class. Each student briefs a portion of the exercise.
Audience:	Entry-level analysts and personnel dealing with the terrorist problem within the intelligence and Law Enforcement Communities. This course is appropriate for those in the first year of a counterterrorism intelligence assignment.
Clearance:	TOP SECRET/SCI
Prerequisites:	Must perform analytical duties in intelligence or law enforcement.
Length:	2 weeks
Frequency:	4 classes per year
Capacity:	Varies
Location:	JMITC, Bolling AFB, MD
VTC:	NONE
Distance Learning:	NONE
Cost:	Per diem and travel to the training location.
Funding:	By parent organization
Curriculum Manager:	JMITC, DAJ-1
CMDSN:	428-2791
CMCOMM:	(202) 231-2791
CMDSNFAX:	428-8497
CMCOMMFAX:	(202) 231-8497
CMCOMME-Mail:	
Scheduling Activity:	JMITC, DAJ-2C
SADSN:	428-3108
SACOMM:	(202) 231-3108
SADSNFAX:	418-2810
SACOMMFAX:	(202) 231-3108
SACOMME-Mail:	
Reviewing Activity:	DIA/JMITC

Title:	**COUNTERINTELLIGENCE ANALYTIC METHODS COURSE (CAMC)**
UJTL Reference:	SN.3
Course Number:	N/A
Objective:	To become familiar with multidiscipline CI analysis; to be able to apply basic tools appropriately; to define Deception and its role; to know locations of CI data bases, and to know how to gather information appropriate to CI reports and products.
Description:	This course provides the analyst with basic tools for multidisciplinary, counterintelligence analysis. Upon completion of the course, the student will better understand how to sort raw reporting in terms of answers to the questions who, what, when, how many and why. The student will learn how to depict counterintelligence and threat components of the decision maker's area of responsibility in terms of population, industry, utilities, agriculture, foreign intelligence and security services, police, religious groups or organizations, and terrorist activity. Students are taught how to construct a matrix that depicts relationships among foreign intelligence service, dissident or other counterintelligence related threats to the force. Students will learn to construct link diagrams depicting these relationships and will practice recognizing and reporting FISS modus operandi patterns emerging therefrom. Students are taught to spot vulnerabilities from patterns in US predeployment and deployment activities as well.
Audience:	Counterintelligence analysts.
Clearance:	TOP SECRET/SI/TK
Prerequisites:	Currently occupy a CI analyst or CI agent position; possess a basic working knowledge of the hostile intelligence threat.
Length:	1 week
Frequency:	3 classes per year
Capacity:	24 students per class
Location:	JMITC, Bolling AFB, MD
VTC:	NONE
Distance Learning:	NONE
Cost:	Per diem and travel to the training location.
Funding:	By parent organization
Curriculum Manager:	JMITC, DAJ-1C
CMDSN:	428-2791
CMCOMM:	(202) 231-2791
CMDSNFAX:	428-8497
CMCOMMFAX:	(202) 231-8497
Scheduling Activity:	JMITC, DAJ-2C
SADSN:	428-3108
SACOMM:	(202) 231-3108
SADSNFAX:	428-2810
SACOMMFAX:	(202) 231-3108
Reviewing Activity:	DIA/JMITC

Title:	**INTERSERVICE SPACE FUNDAMENTALS COURSE**
UJTL Reference:	SN.3
Course Number:	V30ZP13S3 000
Objective:	Familiarization course designed to provide space fundamentals training for individuals with newly assigned duties in non-operator positions involving space operations who require a basic knowledge of space.
Description:	The training scope includes space environment, orbital mechanics, space policy/doctrine/law, satellite and rocket theory, US/CIS missile and satellite systems, rest of world space systems, national and DOD space-related organizations, space control and surveillance systems, command operations and tactical applications of space assets.
Audience:	0-6 and below and civilian equivalents.
Clearance:	SECRET
Prerequisites:	NONE (Personnel with one or more years of space operations experience may find this course does not meet their needs.)
Length:	2 weeks
Frequency:	10 classes per year
Capacity:	20 students
Location:	Colorado Springs, CO
VTC:	NONE
Distance Learning:	NONE
Cost:	Per diem and travel to training location.
Funding:	By parent location
Curriculum Manager:	533 TRS (POC: Mr. Ross Wroblewski)
CMDSN:	275-2686
CMCOMM:	(805) 734-2686
CMDSNFAX:	275-0626
CMCOMMFAX:	(805) 734-0626
CMCOMME-Mail:	wroblepr@aetc7204a.vafb.af.mil
Scheduling Activity:	533 TRS
SADSN:	275-2686
SACOMM:	(805) 734-0626
SADSNFAX:	275-0626
SACOMMFAX:	(805) 734-0626
SACOMME-Mail:	wroblepr@aetc7204a.vafb.af.mil
Reviewing Activity:	N/A

Title:	**JOINT TASK FORCE COMMANDER'S HANDBOOK FOR PEACE OPERATIONS**
UJTL Reference:	SN.8; ST.8
Course Number:	N/A
Objective:	Designed as a resource tool to assist joint force commanders and their staffs in conducting peace operations.
Description:	The handbook provides information to the joint force commander and his staff to assist in the planning and execution of peace operations, as well as humanitarian operations that will likely be conducted in concert with peace operations. The handbook provides information on mission planning, civil-military relationships, joint task force organization and staffing, joint task force commander responsibilities, negotiation and mediation, joint military commissions, transition planning, legal responsibilities, force protection, training requirements, and refugee, displaced person, or migrant camp operations. There is also information concerning the peculiar logistic, intelligence, public affairs, and command and control requirements for peace operations. Though consistent with joint and Service doctrine, it is not a doctrinal publication. Joint Publication 3-07.3, "Joint Tactics, Techniques, and Procedures for Peace Operations" contains joint doctrine for peace operations.
Audience:	Senior commanders designated or about to be named as joint task force commanders for peace operations are the primary audience. The publication is also applicable to anyone participating in peace operations.
Clearance:	N/A
Prerequisites:	NONE
Length:	N/A
Frequency:	N/A
Capacity:	N/A
Location:	N/A
VTC:	N/A
Distance Learning:	See http://www.dtic.mil/doctrine/jel/research_pubs.htm
Cost:	N/A
Funding:	N/A
Curriculum Manager:	USJFCOM JWFC Joint Doctrine Division (LtCol P.S. Vercruysse)
CMDSN:	680-6550
CMCOMM:	(757) 726-6550
CMDSNFAX:	680-6552
CMCOMMFAX:	(757) 726-6552
CMCOMME-Mail:	vercruyp@jwfc.js.mil
Scheduling Activity:	N/A
SADSN:	N/A
SACOMM:	N/A
SADSNFAX:	N/A
SACOMMFAX:	N/A
SACOMME-Mail:	N/A
Reviewing Activity:	N/A

Title:	**MOBILE COUNTERINTELLIGENCE COURSE (MCIC)**
UJTL Reference:	SN.3
Course Number:	N/A
Objective:	Each student will be familiar with the national and DOD all-source CI analytical community and with CI analytic methods.
Description:	Designed to improve the all-source counterintelligence analyst's under-standing of resources available in the community. The course provides instruction on national counterintelligence policy, priorities, organizations, operations, and funding, and on the multidiscipline hostile intelligence threat. Describes and examines various analytical methods and includes brief practical exercises to reinforce these methods.
Audience:	Primarily for military or civilian personnel who perform counterintelligence functions.
Clearance:	SECRET/US Only
Prerequisites:	Limited to personnel currently occupying a Counterintelligence Analyst or Special Agent position with a verifiable job-related requirement to attend the instruction. Non-CI personnel will find this course of limited utility.
Length:	2 or 3 days
Frequency:	As required/requested
Capacity:	Minimum of 20 students; maximum of 50 students
Location:	JMITC, Bolling AFB, MD
VTC:	NONE
Distance Learning:	MTT to requesting organization location
Cost:	TDY and per diem for instructors.
Funding:	Requestor/sponsor fund cites required NLT 30 days prior to MTT departure for CONUS and 45 days for OCONUS training requests.
Curriculum Manager:	JMITC, DAJ-1C
CMDSN:	428-3286
CMCOMM:	(202) 231-3286
CMDSNFAX:	428-2753
CMCOMMFAX:	(202) 231-2753
CMCOMME-Mail:	
Scheduling Activity:	JMITC, DAJ-1
SADSN:	428-3286
SACOMM:	(202) 231-3286
SADSNFAX:	428-2753
SACOMMFAX:	(202) 231-2753
SACOMME-Mail:	
Reviewing Activity:	DIA/JMITC

Title:	**MULTIDISCIPLINE COUNTERINTELLIGENCE COURSE (MDCIC)**
UJTL Reference:	SN.3, SN.2
Course Number:	N/A
Objective:	To know the all-source counterintelligence environment at the national and DOD levels; know the availability of, and how to gain access to all-source CI information and resources in both DOD and the national intelligence community.
Description:	This intensive professional development course builds upon and augments basic CI training provided by the military services or the parent federal agency. The MDCIC improves the professional counterintelligence (CI) officer's understanding of the multidisciplinary approach to CI by direct exposure to national and departmental experts and their products. The course provides instruction each of four objective areas and demonstrates the positive impact on CI activities of an interservice and interdepartmental network of CI professionals who consult among themselves. It emphasizes that today's CI products and operations depend on fusion of information and effort.
Audience:	Counterintelligence professionals (E-6 and above).
Clearance:	TOP SECRET/SCI/TK
Prerequisites:	Currently occupy a CI Analyst or CI Agent position, or have a current job-related requirement to have a MDCI background. Possess a basic, working knowledge of the hostile intelligence threat. This is not an entry-level course; it is designed for journeymen-level CI analysts and special agents.
Length:	2 weeks
Frequency:	3 classes per year
Capacity:	Varies
Location:	JMITC, Bolling AFB, MD
VTC:	NONE
Distance Learning:	NONE
Cost:	Per diem and travel to the training location.
Funding:	By parent organization
Curriculum Manager:	JMITC,DAJ-1
CMDSN:	428-2791
CMCOMM:	(202) 231-2791
CMDSNFAX:	428-8497
CMCOMMFAX:	(202) 231-8497
CMCOMME-Mail:	
Scheduling Activity:	JMITC, DAJ-2C
SADSN:	428-3108
SACOMM:	(202) 231-3108
SADSNFAX:	428-2810
SACOMMFAX:	(202) 231-2810
SACOMME-Mail:	
Reviewing Activity:	JMITC

Title:	**SPACE APPLICATIONS ADVANCED COURSE (SAAC)**
UJTL Reference:	SN 3; OP 3, OP 6
Course Number:	N/A
Objective:	Provides training to Space Support Team members and selected staff personnel pertaining to the effective exploitation and combat application of DOD, Civil, Commercial, and National space systems.
Description:	The course provides in-depth instruction on space system capabilities, applications and support coordination considerations. Training includes blocks of instruction on Theater Air Operations, Space Fundamentals, Environmental Systems, Navigation Systems, Communications Systems, Surveillance and Warning Systems, Space Applications Integration, US National Systems, and a Space Applications Scenario.
Audience:	Personnel identified as Space Support Team members or Space War-fare Center (SWC), Unified or Component Space Commands. No restrictions on rank or service.
Clearance:	TOP SECRET/SCI
Prerequisites:	NONE
Length:	14 days
Frequency:	6 times per year
Capacity:	30 students per course
Location:	Falcon AFB, CO
VTC:	NONE
Distance Learning:	NONE
Cost:	Per diem and travel to the training location.
Funding:	By parent organization
Curriculum Manager:	SWC/DOT (POC: Maj Snell)
CMDSN:	560-9393
CMCOMM:	(719) 567-9393
CMDSNFAX:	560-9591
CMCOMMFAX:	(719) 567-9591
CMCOMME-Mail:	snellke@fafb.af.mil
Scheduling Activity:	SWC/DOT registrars
SADSN:	560-9640/8610/9645
SACOMM:	(719) 567-9640/8610/9645
SADSNFAX:	560-9591
SACOMMFAX:	(719) 567-9591
SACOMME-Mail:	registr@fafb.af.mil
Reviewing Activity:	N/A

Title:	**SPACE APPLICATIONS SENIOR OFFICER COURSE (SASOC)**
UJTL Reference:	SN.3; OP 3, OP 6
Course Number:	N/A
Objective:	Provides senior officer training pertaining to the effective exploitation and combat application of DOD, Civil, Commercial, and National space systems.
Description:	This "accelerated" course provides an overview of DOD, Civil, Commercial, and National space systems, and the integration of their out-puts/products into theater operations in support of campaign and operations planning and theater battle management. Training includes blocks of instruction on space fundamentals, environmental systems, navigation systems, communications systems, surveillance and warning systems, space applications integration and US national systems.
Audience:	Normally 0-6 and above.
Clearance:	TOP SECRET/SCI
Prerequisites:	NONE
Length:	Two days
Frequency:	Eight times per year
Capacity:	15 students per course
Location:	Falcon AFB, CO
VTC:	NONE
Distance Learning:	NONE
Cost:	Per diem and travel to the training location.
Funding:	By parent organization
Curriculum Manager:	SWC/DOT (POC: Capt Smith)
CMDSN:	560-9658
CMCOMM:	(719) 567-9658
CMDSNFAX:	560-9591
CMCOMMFAX:	(719) 567-9591
CMCOMME-Mail:	smithwm@ffb.mil
Scheduling Activity:	SWC/DOT Registrar
SADSN:	560-9640/8610/9645
SACOMM:	(719) 567-9591
SADSNFAX:	560-9591
SACOMMFAX:	(719) 567-9591
SACOMME-Mail:	registr@fafb.af.mil
Reviewing Activity:	N/A

Title:	**TERRORISM: GROUP DYNAMICS ANALYSIS (TERR1) - VTC**
UJTL Reference:	SN.3, SN.2; ST.2, ST.8
Course Number:	N/A
Objective:	To provide an overview of international terrorism and the response of the US counterterrorist community.
Description:	Course content varies depending on what is currently happening at the time of the broadcast. Standard topics include latest statistics on international terrorism, issues of concern to the US government, and recent intelligence community publications.
Audience:	Any intelligence professional.
Clearance:	UNCLASSIFIED
Prerequisites:	NONE
Length:	1 1/2 hours
Frequency:	As required/requested
Capacity:	As determined by requestor
Location:	JMITC, Bolling AFB, MD
VTC:	Yes
Distance Learning:	NONE
Cost:	Requestor coordinates times between VTC delivery and receive location.
Funding:	By requestor
Curriculum Manager:	JMITC, DAJ-1
CMDSN:	428-3286
CMCOMM:	(202) 231-3286
CMDSNFAX:	428-2753
CMCOMMFAX:	(202) 231-2753
CMCOMME-Mail:	
Scheduling Activity:	JMITC, DAJ-1
SADSN:	428-3286
SACOMM:	(202) 231-3286
SADSNFAX:	428-2753
SACOMMFAX	(202) 231-2753
SACOMME-Mail:	
Reviewing Activity:	DIA/JMITC

Title:	**CONTINGENCY WARTIME PLANNING COURSE**
UJTL Reference:	SN.5; ST.5
Course Number:	MCADRE002 PDS Code 82U
Objective:	Instruct all skills in the complicated process of Deliberate and Crisis Action Planning.
Description:	The curriculum consists of five blocks of instruction covering the following aspects of planning: players, systems, planning, execution, and analysis. It includes important features of the Planning process; emphasizes Air Force 10-series publications, the Joint Operation Planning and Execution System (JOPES), and the USAF War and Mobilization Plan (WMP); deals with Time-Phased Force and Deployment Data (TPFDD), and the Air Force Contingency Operation/Mobility Planning and Execution System (COMPES); contains a series of exercises designed to reinforce academic presentations. The exercises address such topics as TPFDD development, concept of operation process, support force planning, OPLAN development, and base support planning.
Audience:	War planners in grades E-5 through 0-5, and civilian equivalents the basic of Air Force planning. CWPC is one of the formal courses identified by the Air Staff as a prerequisite for the award of the "R" prefix to Air Force Specialty Codes.
Clearance:	SECRET
Prerequisites:	Air Force officers and NCOs in the grades E-5 through O-5, and equivalent civilian grades, en route or assigned to staff contingency or wartime planning functions at wing level or above. Requests for attendance by personnel of other Services will be considered on an individual basis by the department chairman.
Length:	3 weeks
Frequency:	9 classes per year
Capacity:	630 students per year
Location:	Maxwell AFB, AL
VTC:	NONE
Distance Learning:	NONE
Cost:	Lodging plus per diem.
Funding:	The course is a mixture of AU funded quotas and Unit funded quotas.
Curriculum Manager:	Mr. Ken Hill
CMDSN:	493-2638
CMCOMM:	(334) 953-2638
CMDSNFAX:	493-4336
CMCOMMFAX:	(334) 953-4336
Scheduling Activity:	Mr. Ken Hill
SADSN:	493-2638
SACOMM:	(334) 953-2638
SADSNFAX:	493-4336
SACOMMFAX:	(334) 953-4336
Reviewing Activity:	N/A

Title:	**NAVAL COMMAND COLLEGE**
UJTL Reference:	SN.5
Course Number:	S-00-1202
Objective:	Assists specially selected international senior naval officers to prepare themselves for higher command responsibilities in their own navies, through education in planning, decision making, and strategic analysis. To strengthen association and understanding between US and international officers and to familiarize them with US democratic institutions and US military organization, methods, and doctrine, particularly those of the US Navy. To foster friendship, knowledge, and cooperation among the friendly and allied navies from around the world.
Description:	Completely integrated with US College of Naval Warfare officers and civilians for three major study areas. Also includes Defense Information Program and Invitational Program Visits to support the academic regimen and to expose students to the economic, industrial, governmental, cultural, and geographic diversity of the US beyond those presented in Newport, RI. Major study areas, conducted at the graduate level, are: Strategy and Policy; National Security Decision Making; and Joint Military Operations.
Audience:	International naval officers O-5 to O-6.
Clearance:	N/A
Prerequisites:	English language competence, invitation by CNO.
Length:	44 weeks
Frequency:	1 session per year (begins in August)
Capacity:	35 students per session
Location:	Newport, RI
VTC:	NONE
Distance Learning:	NONE
Cost:	Home navy agreement.
Funding:	Home navy agreement.
Curriculum Manager:	Naval War College (POC: CAPT Bixler)
CMDSN:	N/A
CMCOMM:	(401) 841-2245
CMDSNFAX:	N/A
CMCOMMFAX:	(401) 841-3647
CMCOMME-Mail:	
Scheduling Activity:	Naval War College (POC: CDR Demming)
SADSN:	N/A
SACOMM:	(401) 841-2074
SADSNFAX:	N/A
SACOMMFAX:	(401) 841-3647
SACOMME-Mail:	
Reviewing Activity:	N/A

Title:	**NAVAL STAFF COLLEGE**
UJTL Reference:	SN.5
Course Number:	S-00-1203
Objective:	Assists specially selected international mid-grade naval officers to prepare themselves for higher command responsibilities in their own navies, through education in planning, decision making, and strategic analysis. To strengthen association and understanding between US and international officers and to familiarize them with US democratic institutions and US military organization, methods, and doctrine, particularly those of the US Navy. To foster friendship, knowledge and cooperation among the friendly and allied navies from around the world.
Description:	Provides a condensed and modified version of the US College of Naval Command and Staff curriculum. Designed to enhance the under-standing of national security decision making and maritime operations, and the decision making abilities of students. Major study areas include: Strategy and Policy; National Security Decision Making; Joint Maritime Operations; and International Law and Ocean Policy.
Audience:	International naval officers O-3 to O-4.
Clearance:	N/A
Prerequisites:	English language competence, invitation by CNO.
Length:	23 weeks
Frequency:	2 classes per year convening in January and July.
Capacity:	25 students per class
Location:	Newport, RI
VTC:	NONE
Distance Learning:	NONE
Cost:	Home navy agreement.
Funding:	Home navy agreement.
Curriculum Manager:	Naval War College (POC: CAPT Odegaard)
CMDSN:	N/A
CMCOMM:	(401) 841-2010
CMDSNFAX:	N/A
CMCOMMFAX:	(401) 841-3579
CMCOMME-Mail:	
Scheduling Activity:	Naval War College (POC: Mrs. Deery)
SADSN:	N/A
SACOMM:	(401) 841-2074
SADSNFAX:	N/A
SACOMMFAX:	(401) 841-3579
SACOMME-Mail:	
Reviewing Activity:	N/A

Title:	**FLAG AND GENERAL OFFICER SEMINAR (FGOS)**
UJTL Reference:	SN.5, SN.1; ST.5
Course Number:	N/A
Objective:	For each participant to gain familiarity with the joint planning process in accordance with the Joint Operation Planning and Execution System (JOPES), and proposed changes to the process.
Description:	Seminar participants are introduced to the historical development of JOPES and its associated automated support. The interrelationship between JOPES and the Joint Strategic Planning System (JSPS) and the Planning, Programming, and Budget System (PPBS) is identified. Seminar participants discuss plan development, including the construction of Time Phased Force and Deployment Data (TPFDD) in both peacetime and crisis situations; the link between deliberate and crisis planning; and actions to improve joint planning and execution. Through-out the seminar, capabilities and limitations of current planning and execution systems are highlighted.
Audience:	0-6 and above/SES.
Clearance:	NONE
Prerequisites:	NONE
Length:	2 hours
Frequency:	The FGOS is normally presented in conjunction with the Joint Planning Orientation Course (JPOC).
Capacity:	Seminars are generally small. Attendance is not limited.
Location:	AFSC, Norfolk, VA
VTC:	In development
Distance Learning:	The JPOC is presented at least twice annually at each of the combatant commands; four times annually in the Washington, D.C. area, and four times annually at the AFSC on weekends to support other requirements.
Cost:	NONE
Funding:	AFSC
Curriculum Manager:	AFSC (POC: LTC Antis; Ms. DeGeere; Mr. Rowse)
CMDSN:	564-5386
CMCOMM:	(757) 444-5386
CMDSNFAX:	564-5317
CMCOMMFAX:	(757) 444-5317
CMCOMME-Mail:	
Scheduling Activity:	Armed Forces Staff College (POC: Ms. DeGeere; Mr. Rowse)
SADSN:	564-5386
SACOMM:	(757) 444-5386
SADSNFAX:	564-5317
SACOMMFAX:	(757) 444-5317
SACOMME-Mail:	
Reviewing Activity:	N/A

Title:	**MILITARY FAMILIARIZATION COURSE FOR CIVILIAN INTELLIGENCE ANALYSTS (MILFAM)**
UJTL Reference:	SN.7, SN.2, SN.3
Course Number:	N/A
Objective:	To familiarize civilian intelligence analysts with the US National Military Command Structures, Armed Forces, and joint military planning process.
Description:	Introduces the student to the US National Military Command Structure. Students will learn the process of how National Military Strategy is translated into military forces for use with contingency plans using JOPES. Students will become familiar with DOD, Joint Staff, Unified Commanders', and Services' roles in projecting military power. Included in the training is an introduction to the Services' missions, structures, doctrines, and force capabilities, as well as how CINCs fight using a JTF. At the end of the course, students should understand how military planners do their jobs, how the US structures combat forces to fight, and what types of intelligence are needed by military planners to support force contingencies.
Audience:	Civilians in grade GS-8 to GS-13.
Clearance:	SECRET/NOFORN
Prerequisites:	Civilian intelligence analysts in grades GS-8 to GS-13 with no or limited military experience who need an understanding of the basic structure and workings of the US Armed Forces and the military planning process.
Length:	3 days
Frequency:	3 classes per year
Capacity:	Varies
Location:	JMITC, Bolling AFB, MD
VTC:	NONE
Distance Learning:	NONE
Cost:	Per diem and travel to the training location.
Funding:	By parent organization
Curriculum Manager:	JMITC, DAJ-1
CMDSN:	428-2791
CMCOMM:	(202) 231-2791
CMDSNFAX:	428-8497
CMCOMMFAX:	(202) 231-8497
CMCOMME-Mail:	
Scheduling Activity:	JMITC, DAJ-2C
SADSN:	428-3108
SACOMM:	(202) 231-3108
SADSNFAX:	428-2810
SACOMMFAX:	(202) 231-2810
SACOMME-Mail:	
Reviewing Activity:	DIA/JMITC

Title:	**FINANCIAL MANAGEMENT OF INTELLIGENCE (FMIT)**
UJTL Reference:	SN.7, SN.2
Course Number:	N/A
Objective:	To know the fundamentals of intelligence financial management, the latest developments in the federal budget process, and how these changes have affected financial management in the DOD and the Intelligence Community.
Description:	Examines the two principle resource management systems of interest to intelligence professionals, i.e., the Capabilities Programming and Budgeting System (CPBS) used by the Director of Central Intelligence to manage the resources of the National Foreign Intelligence Program (NFIP), and the Planning, Programming, and Budgeting System (PPBS) used by the Secretary of Defense to manage resources of the DOD. Also examined are: (a) the major component programs of the NFIP, with emphasis on the General Defense Intelligence Program (GDIP); (b) Tactical Intelligence and Related Activities (TIARA); (c) The Five Year Defense Program (FYDP); (d) the Congressional Budget Process; (e) budgetary aspects of congressional oversight of intelligence; and (f) the execution of the federal budget.
Audience:	Military and civilian personnel within the Intelligence Community having budgetary responsibility, including department heads in any intelligence organization. This is a particularly appropriate course for those dealing with, or assigned to, intelligence financial management functions and activities.
Clearance:	TOP SECRET/SCI
Prerequisites:	NONE
Length:	1 week
Frequency:	Varies
Capacity:	Varies
Location:	JMITC, Bolling AFB, MD
VTC:	Some VTC delivery possible
Distance Learning:	NONE
Cost:	Per diem and travel to the training location.
Funding:	By parent organization
Curriculum Manager:	JMITC, DAJ-1
CMDSN:	243-2791
CMCOMM:	(202) 373-2791
CMDSNFAX:	243-8497
CMCOMMFAX:	(202) 373-8497
CMCOMME-Mail:	
Scheduling Activity:	JMITC, DAJ-2C
SADSN:	243-3108
SACOMM:	(202) 373-3108
SADSNFAX:	243-2810
SACOMMFAX:	(202) 373-2810
SACOMME-Mail:	
Reviewing Activity:	DIA/JMI

Title:	**NATIONAL INTELLIGENCE COURSE (NIC)**
UJTL Reference:	SN.7, SN.2, SN.3
Course Number:	N/A
Objective:	To know the missions, functions, and organizations of national and joint intelligence activities, both civilian and military.
Description:	This is an entry-level course for personnel newly assigned to the US Intelligence Community. The course covers the intelligence cycles; overview of intelligence disciplines; fundamentals of strategic intelligence; National Foreign Intelligence Community; and appraisal of current threats to the US Students will be better prepared to meet worldwide challenges to US national security interests.
Audience:	Personnel in grades O-1 through O-3; E-4 through E-6; or GS-05 through GS-09 who are or will be associated with the intelligence process.
Clearance:	SECRET
Prerequisites:	Non-intelligence professionals assigned to intelligence units.
Length:	1 week
Frequency:	8 classes per year
Capacity:	Varies
Location:	JMITC, Bolling AFB, MD
VTC:	NONE
Distance Learning:	NONE
Cost:	Per diem and travel to the training location.
Funding:	By parent organization
Curriculum Manager:	JMITC, DAJ-1
CMDSN:	428-2791
CMCOMM:	(202) 231-2791
CMDSNFAX:	428-8497
CMCOMMFAX:	(202) 231-8497
CMCOMME-Mail:	
Scheduling Activity:	JMITC, DAJ-2C
SADSN:	428-3108
SACOMM:	(202) 231-3108
SADSNFAX:	428-2810
SACOMMFAX:	(202) 231-2810
SACOMME-Mail:	
Reviewing Activity:	DIA/JMITC

Title:	**AIR DEPLOYMENT PLANNING COURSE (ADPC)**
UJTL Reference:	ST.1
Course Number:	8C-S135/553-F
Objective:	To provide selected personnel from all four military services (active and reserve) and DOD civilians with a working knowledge of planning, organizing, and conducting unit air movements training and/or operations. Course graduates receive a 2 year air load planning certification.
Description:	Instruction for personnel on the responsibilities of unit air movements; strategic airlift operations overview; automated air movement documentation systems; hazardous cargo by air; planning operations and manifesting; preparation of equipment and personnel; 463L pallet cargo system; weighing; marking and determining C/B of cargo; joint inspection; loading and restraint fundamentals; A/DACG procedures; aircraft characteristics and limitations; marshaling and staging procedures; civil reserve air fleet; marshaling safety; aircraft configurations; unit air movements planning; and air loadout procedures. Throughout the course, students participate in numerous practical exercises and hands-on training to reinforce learning objectives.
Audience:	0-1 to 0-4; WO's; E-4 and up; DOD civilians.
Clearance:	NONE
Prerequisites:	Individuals should be appointed or under consideration for appointment to a unit, staff, or installation movement position involving strategic airlift operations.
Length:	3 weeks
Frequency:	7 classes per year
Capacity:	30 students per class
Location:	Ft. Eustis, VA
VTC:	NONE
Distance Learning:	Capability to conduct a two week mobile training course
Cost:	Per diem and travel to the training location. Per diem and travel for Mobile Training Team if requested.
Funding:	By parent organization
Curriculum Manager:	USA Transportation Center and School (POC: CPT Bowes)
CMDSN:	927-2120
CMCOMM:	(757) 878-2120
CMDSNFAX:	927-4900
CMCOMMFAX:	(757) 878-4900
CMCOMME-MAIL:	
Scheduling Activity:	ATRRS
SADSN:	927-2039
SACOMM:	(757) 878-2039
SADSNFAX:	927-4900
SACOMMFAX:	(757) 878-4900
SACOMME-MAIL:	
Reviewing Activity:	SACS

Title:	**JOINT AEROSPACE COMMAND AND CONTROL COURSE (JAC2C)**
UJTL Reference:	ST.5; OP.5
Course Number:	N/A
Objective:	Prepares selected officers, senior NCOs, and DOD civilians to plan, produce, and execute an Air Tasking Order (ATO) in support of a Joint Task Force.
Description:	This course focuses on battle management process required to plan, produce, and execute an Air Tasking Order and integrate air and surface resources into joint combat operations in a theater battle. The course follows a process including lectures, seminars, hands-on computer activities, and an end-of-course command and control (C2) exercise. The course covers basic doctrine, mission, and organization of the services; command, control, and communications systems; intelligence support capabilities; tactical missions and major weapons systems used in joint operations; capabilities and limitations of command and control warfare (C2W) concepts/strategy; and the CTAPS computer tools used in current operations.
Audience:	Students should be field grade or senior company grade officers, senior NCOs (E-7 and above), or civilians assigned to DOD agencies or employed by defense industries. International students can occasionally be admitted.
Clearance:	SECRET
Prerequisites:	Students require an in-depth understanding of the Theater Air Ground System (TAGS) or current CTAPS computer tools to perform their duties to plan, publish, and execute an ATO/Airspace Control Order (ACO).
Length:	17 days
Frequency:	7 classes per year
Capacity:	94 students per class
Location:	Hurlburt Field, FL
VTC:	NONE
Distance Learning:	NONE
Cost:	Per diem and travel to the training location.
Funding:	By parent organization
Curriculum Manager:	USAFBTS/DAI (Maj Jones)
CMDSN:	579-6286
CMCOMM:	(850) 884-6286
CMDSNFAX:	579-5550
CMCOMMFAX:	(850) 884-5550
CMCOMME-MAIL:	jones.kenneth@jfacc.hurlburt.af.mil
Scheduling Activity:	USAFBTS/DSSF
SADSN:	579-6237
SACOMM:	(850) 884-6237
SADSNFAX:	579-5399
SACOMMFAX:	(850) 884-5399
SACOMME-MAIL:	
Reviewing Activity:	USAFBTS

Title:	**JOINT AEROSPACE COMPUTER APPLICATIONS COURSE (JACAC)**
UJTL Reference:	ST.5; OP.5
Course Number:	N/A
Objective:	Provides the fundamentals of Contingency Theater Automated Planning System (CTAPS) operations.
Description:	The course teaches three tracks. The Operations Track focuses on the CTAPS/Computer-Assisted Force Management System (CAFMS) module which normally is used to execute and monitor missions in the AOC, Air Support Operations Center (ASOC), Control and Reporting Center (CRC), or Wing Operations Center (WOC). The Plans Track focuses on the CTAPS/Advance Planning System (APS) module used to train the individuals involved with the entering of data to APS for the purpose of developing an Air Tasking Order (ATO). The Intelligence Track focuses on CTAPS/Combat Intelligence System (CIS) and Rapid Application of Air Power (RAAP) with the concept of adding and monitoring data to assist planners and operator.
Audience:	Individuals attending the course will normally be assigned duties at an AOC, Battlefield Coordination Detachment (BCD), CRC, ASOC, WOC, or other theater air ground system agency, command, or element.
Clearance:	SECRET
Prerequisites:	Students should be prepared to attend tracks according to their area of expertise and be assigned to organizations which require an in-depth understanding of the current CTAPS computer programs.
Length:	4 days
Frequency:	8 classes per year
Capacity:	Normally 50 students per class
Location:	Hurlburt Field, FL
VTC:	NONE
Distance Learning:	NONE
Cost:	Per diem and travel to the training location.
Funding:	By parent organization
Curriculum Manager:	USAFBTS/DAI (Maj Roberts)
CMDSN:	579-6229
CMCOMM:	(850) 884-6229
CMDSNFAX:	579-5550
CMCOMMEFAX:	(850) 884-5550
CMCOMME-MAIL:	roberts.glenn@jfacc.hurlburt.af.mil
Scheduling Activity:	USAFBTS/DSSF
SADSN:	579-6237
SACOMM:	(850) 884-6237
SADSNFAX:	579-5399
SACOMMEFAX:	(850) 884-5399
SACOMME-MAIL:	
Reviewing Activity:	USAFBTS

Title:	**JOINT AEROSPACE ADMINISTRATOR COURSE (JASAC)** ST.5; OP.5
UJTL Reference:	N/A
Course Number:	
Objective:	To train selected individuals in the fundamentals of UNIX, TCP/IP networking and communications protocols, relational databases, and Contingency Theater Automated Planning System (CTAPS) systems administration.
Description:	JASAC has four blocks of instructions: UNIX, ORACLE/SYBASE, CTAPS, and Wing Command and Control System (WCCS). The WCCS track is taught only three times a year. This course focuses on those individuals assigned system administration duties within the Joint Air Operations Center (JAOC), or related Joint organizations or facilities. The course ends with a 3-day CTAPS/WCCS/CIS combined class exercise.
Audience:	Focuses on those individuals assigned system administration duties within the AOC, Numbered Air Forces (NAFs), Composite Wings, or related joint organizations or facilities.
Clearance:	SECRET
Prerequisites:	Students must have an introduction to UNIX completed prior to attendance and be assigned to organizations which require an in-depth understanding of the UNIX systems administration, which may include knowledge of current CTAPS, WCCS, or CIS computer programs.
Length:	15 days (course projected to go to 46 days May 99)
Frequency:	5 classes per year.
Capacity:	50 students per class.
Location:	Hurlburt Field, FL
VTC:	NONE
Distance Learning:	NONE
Cost:	Per diem and travel to the training location.
Funding:	By parent organization
Curriculum Manager:	USAFBTS/DSC (1LT Allen)
CMDSN:	579-2527
CMCOMM:	(850) 884-2527
CMDSNFAX:	579-6743
CMCOMMFAX:	(850) 884-6743
CMCOMME-MAIL:	allen.gary@jfacc.hurlburt.af.mil
Scheduling Activity:	USAFBTS/DSSF
SADSN:	579-6237
SACOMM:	(850) 884-6237
SADSNFAX:	579-5399
SACOMMFAX:	(850) 884-5399
CMCOMME-MAIL:	
Reviewing Activity:	USAFBTS

Title:	**JOINT COMBAT SEARCH AND RESCUE (JCSAR) COORDINATOR COURSE**
UJTL Reference:	ST.4; OP.4; TA.6
Course Number:	E5AZG1C371 002, PDS Code 7G5
Objective:	To introduce concepts, doctrine, and procedures for combat search and rescue mission management based upon JCS 3-50.XX-series publications.
Description:	The course encompasses CSAR definitions, benefits, and types; isolated personnel profiles, legal status, and responsibilities; US military service organization and missions; CSAR and joint battlefield management involving the Air Operations Center, Special Instructions, Air Tasking Order, and SAR duty officers; search and rescue center organization, missions, set-up, and documentation; CSAR stages, mission planning factors, and recovery options; multi-service CSAR policy and resources; coordinate plotting systems and search patterns; intelligence, reconnaissance, and threat definitions, types, and reports; and CSAR scenarios.
Audience:	Designed for US military personnel , all grades, (Air Force: AFSCs 1C3XX—enlisted; 13BXX—command and control officers), primarily those en route to worldwide search and rescue centers, CSAR contingency operations, CSAR exercise positions or CSAR-related duties.
Clearance:	NONE
Prerequisites:	NONE
Length:	4 days
Frequency:	4 classes per year.
Capacity:	15-20 students per class
Location:	Hurlburt Field, FL
VTC:	NONE
Distance Learning:	NONE
Cost:	Per diem and travel to the training location.
Funding:	By parent organization
Curriculum Manager:	USAFBTS/DAJ (Maj Bloser)
CMDSN:	579-7638
CMCOMM:	(850) 884-7638
CMDSNFAX:	579-5550
CMCOMMFAX:	(850) 884-5550
CMCOMME-MAIL:	bloser.richard@jfacc.hurlburt.af.mil
Scheduling Activity:	AFRCC/RCS (HQ ACC)
SADSN:	574-9990 (ask for connection to 898-2273)
SACOMM:	(757) 898-2273
SADSNFAX:	
SACOMMFAX:	
SACOMME-MAIL:	
Reviewing Activity:	AFRCC/RCS

Title:	**JOINT SPECIAL OPERATIONS INTERMEDIATE SEMINAR (JSOIS)**
UJTL Reference:	ST.1
Course Number:	Pending
Objective:	Know the unique function and interrelationships of a special operations staff, gain an understanding of joint special operations doctrine and the planning process, and to apply the planning process to develop and present courses of action to the decision maker.
Description:	Course is specifically designed for SOF officers, senior NCOs, and USG civilian employee equivalents assigned to or programmed for assignment to a special operations billet. The intent is to provide students en route to Intermediate Service School (ISS) with 2 weeks of joint special operations background to make them better "SOF Ambassadors" while attending ISS and to provide a SOF foundation upon which to build while attending ISS.
Audience:	O-3/O-4, Senior NCOs, and USG civilian equivalents.
Clearance:	TOP SECRET
Prerequisites:	Working knowledge of special operations; completion of Introduction to Special Operations course; Joint Special Operations Staff Officer course; and Joint Special Operations Planning Workshop is desirable.
Length:	10 days
Frequency:	1 class per year
Capacity:	25-30
Location:	Hurlburt Field, FL
VTC:	NONE
Distance Learning:	NONE
Cost:	Per diem and travel to the training location.
Funding:	ISS selectees USAFSOS funded; all others parent organization funded
Curriculum Manager:	USAFSOS (POC: Maj Hondrum)
CMDSN:	579-1842
CMCOMM:	(904) 884-1842
CMDSNFAX:	579-1851
CMCOMMFAX:	(904) 884-1851
CMCOMME-MAIL:	
Scheduling Activity:	USAFSOS (POC: Mrs. Weber)
SADSN:	579-4731
SACOMM:	(904) 884-4731
SADSNFAX:	579-4732
SACOMMFAX:	(904) 884-4732
SACOMME-MAIL:	
Reviewing Activity:	N/A

Title:	**JOINT SPECIAL OPERATIONS PLANNING WORKSHOP (JSOPW)**
UJTL Reference:	ST.1
Course Number:	AFSOC 149002
Objective:	For each student to gain an understanding of the joint special operations planning process and to apply the planning process to develop and present courses of action to the decision maker.
Description:	Seminar with guest speakers as the leaders of each respective class. The course focuses on joint special operations planning and resources, accomplished through course materials, guest speakers, and a three day planning exercise with the class formed into a JSOTF.
Audience:	O-3 and above and civilian equivalent special operations personnel.
Clearance:	TOP SECRET
Prerequisites:	Personnel who need to have a working knowledge of special operations crisis planning. Completion of Introduction to Special Operations Course is desired.
Length:	10 days
Frequency:	4 classes per year
Capacity:	28-30 students per class
Location:	Hurlburt Field, FL
VTC:	NONE
Distance Learning:	NONE
Cost:	Per diem and travel to the training location.
Funding:	By parent organization
Curriculum Manager:	USAFSOS (POC: Capt Meade)
CMDSN:	579-1849
CMCOMM:	(904) 884-1849
CMDSNFAX:	579-7989
CMCOMMFAX:	(904) 884-7989
CMCOMME-MAIL:	
Scheduling Activity:	USAFSOS (POC: Mrs. Weber)
SADSN:	579-4731
SACOMM:	(904) 884-4731
SADSNFAX:	579-4732
SACOMMFAX:	(904) 884-4732
SACOMME-MAIL:	
Reviewing Activity:	N/A

Title:	**MOBILIZATION AND DEPLOYMENT PLANNING COURSE (MDPC)**
UJTL Reference:	ST.1; OP.1; SN.6; SN.1
Course Number:	2G-F65/500-F-1
Objective:	To train Active and Reserve Component Officers, Warrant Officers, Senior NCOs, and DOD civilians to perform the duties of a mobilization staff officer. The course is structured to provide mobilization planners at all levels, from DOD down to the installation, with the basic understanding of the mobilization process and specified procedures for implementation.
Description:	The MDPC is taught in residence at Fort Eustis, VA as part of the Joint Strategic Deployment Training Center (JSDTC). MDPC is arranged and taught in eight blocks of instruction.
Audience:	Military personnel from all Services and foreign military, and DOD civilians.
Clearance:	SECRET
Prerequisites:	Presently performing or about to perform duties as mobilization planners and their supervisors.
Length:	2 weeks
Frequency:	10-11 classes per year
Capacity:	35 students per class
Location:	Ft. Eustis, VA
VTC:	VTC is located on Fort Eustis.
Distance Learning:	NONE
Cost:	Per diem and travel to the training location.
Funding:	By parent organization
Curriculum Manager:	USA Transportation Center and School (POC: LTC Waldron)
CMDSN:	927-6069
CMCOMM:	(757) 878-6069
CMDSNFAX:	927-2841
CMCOMMFAX:	(757) 878-2841
CMCOMME-MAIL:	
Scheduling Activity:	ATOM-O, TRADOC
SADSN:	680-2524
SACOMM:	(757) 727-2524
SADSNFAX:	680-4337
SACOMMFAX:	(757) 727-4337
SACOMME-MAIL:	
Reviewing Activity:	SACS

Title:	**COUNTERDRUG BASIC INTELLIGENCE COURSE (CDI)**
UJTL Reference:	ST.2, ST.8; SN.2, SN.7
Course Number:	J-243-0996
Objective:	Provides law enforcement agency and DOD personnel assigned to counterdrug intelligence fusion activities the basic knowledge to analyze data from available law enforcement agencies and DOD sensors and sources.
Description:	Provides instruction on geopolitical/historical overview, drug production/transportation, organized crime/ trafficking organizations, collection/reporting, DOD and law enforcement operations information systems and databases and tactical fusion center operations.
Audience:	Joint/DOD personnel (E-2 through 0-5) and federal law enforcement agency personnel with little or no experience in conducting counterdrug operations.
Clearance:	SECRET
Prerequisites:	NONE
Length:	5 days
Frequency:	8 classes per year
Capacity:	25 students per class
Location:	NMITC, Dam Neck, VA
VTC:	NONE
Distance Learning:	NONE
Cost:	Per diem and travel to the training location.
Funding:	By parent organization
Curriculum Manager:	NMITC (Lt. Kerschl)
CMDSN:	433-0116
CMCOMM:	(757) 433-0116
CMDSNFAX:	433-0336
CMCOMMFAX:	(757) 433-0336
CMCOMME-MAIL:	
Scheduling Activity:	NMITC
SADSN:	433-0126
SACOMM:	(757) 433-0126
SADSNFAX:	N/A
SACOMMFAX:	N/A
SACOMME-MAIL:	
Reviewing Activity:	CNET

Title:	**EMERALD USER (EMERALD)**
UJTL Reference:	ST.2
Course Number:	J-243-2958
Objective:	Prepares personnel to operate an Emerald workstation.
Description:	Provides instruction on systems overview, the relational database management system, basic operations, data input/retrieval, link analysis, E-mail, and security. Course is run as a workshop with each student operating an Emerald workstation.
Audience:	Federal, state and local law enforcement agency personnel and joint/DOD personnel assigned to the counterdrug intelligence community.
Clearance:	SECRET
Prerequisites:	NONE
Length:	5 days
Frequency:	12 classes per year
Capacity:	10 students per class
Location:	NMITC, Dam Neck, VA
VTC:	NONE
Distance Learning:	NONE
Cost:	Per diem and travel to the training location.
Funding:	By parent organization
Curriculum Manager:	NMITC (Ms. Hunger)
CMDSN:	433-0114
CMCOMM:	(757) 433-0114
CMDSNFAX:	433-0336
CMCOMMFAX:	(757) 433-0336
CMCOMME-MAIL:	
Scheduling Activity:	NMITC
SADSN:	433-0126
SACOMM:	(757) 433-0126
SADSNFAX:	N/A
SACOMMFAX:	N/A
SACOMME-MAIL:	
Reviewing Activity:	CNET

Title:	**EXPEDITIONARY WARFARE INTELLIGENCE COURSE (EWIC)**
UJTL Reference:	ST.2; OP.2
Course Number:	J-150-2966
Objective:	Prepares intelligence personnel to support expeditionary warfare operations.
Description:	Provides advanced instruction on intelligence support to amphibious warfare, NEO, special warfare in support of amphibious operations, and low intensity conflict. Course includes a comprehensive three day practical exercise in which students demonstrate proficiency and understanding of intelligence requirements during contingency planning.
Audience:	Available to all officer and enlisted intelligence personnel E-5 and above.
Clearance:	SECRET (SCI preferred)
Prerequisites:	Collateral duty intelligence personnel must complete. Service basic intelligence training course.
Length:	13-17 days
Frequency:	FITCPAC 5 classes per year. NMITC 4 classes per year.
Capacity:	FITCPAC 25 students per class. NMITC 20 students per class.
Location:	NMITC, Dam Neck, VA
VTC:	NONE
Distance Learning:	NONE
Cost:	Per diem and travel to the training location.
Funding:	By parent organization
Curriculum Manager:	NMITC (PO Dunn)
CMDSN:	433-0020
CMCOMM:	(757) 433-0020
CMDSNFAX:	433-8210
CMCOMMFAX:	(757) 433-8210
CMCOMME-MAIL:	
Scheduling Activity:	NMITC / COMTRAPAC 72
SADSN:	433-0020 / 524-1402
SACOMM:	(757) 433-0020
SADSNFAX:	524-1404
SACOMMFAX:	N/A
SACOMME-MAIL:	
Reviewing Activity:	CNET

Title:	**JOINT INTELLIGENCE CENTER COURSE (JIC)**
UJTL Reference:	ST.2
Course Number:	J-243-0972
Objective:	Prepares intelligence personnel to support the theater Joint Intelligence Center.
Description:	Provides the essential skills required to conduct effective all-source intelligence analysis.
Audience:	Intelligence officers and enlisted personnel E-5 and above assigned to joint intelligence billets.
Clearance:	TOP SECRET/SCI
Prerequisites:	NONE
Length:	26 days
Frequency:	7 classes per year
Capacity:	24 students per class
Location:	NMITC, Dam Neck, VA
VTC:	NONE
Distance Learning:	NONE
Cost:	Per diem and travel to the training location.
Funding:	By parent organization
Curriculum Manager:	NMITC (Lt. Shirer)
CMDSN:	433-0323
CMCOMM:	(757) 433-0323
CMDSNFAX:	433-0336
CMCOMMFAX:	(757) 433-0336
CMCOMME-MAIL:	
Scheduling Activity:	PERS-408C/D
SADSN:	224-3131
SACOMM:	(703) 614-2665
SADSNFAX:	N/A
SACOMMFAX:	N/A
SACOMME-MAIL:	
Reviewing Activity:	CNET

Title:	**NAVAL INTELLIGENCE MID-CAREER COURSE (NIMCC)**
UJTL Reference:	ST.2
Course Number:	J-3A-0998
Objective:	Exposes mid-grade officers to new challenges and emergent ideas and technologies.
Description:	Focuses on topics which provide students with a strategic and national level perspective on military Service intelligence organizations and joint warfare/operations.
Audience:	Mid-grade intelligence officers and enlisted personnel E-8 and above and DOD/DoN civilian personnel GS-11 and above.
Clearance:	TOP SECRET/SCI
Prerequisites:	A 3-5 page unclassified paper on an intelligence related topic to be submitted upon class convening.
Length:	12 days
Frequency:	4 classes per year
Capacity:	30 students per class
Location:	NMITC, Dam Neck, VA
VTC:	NONE
Distance Learning:	NONE
Cost:	Per diem and travel to the training location.
Funding:	By parent organization
Curriculum Manager:	NMITC (Lt Rigazzi)
CMDSN:	433-0019
CMCOMM:	(757) 433-0019
CMDSNFAX:	433-0336
CMCOMMFAX:	(757) 433-0336
CMCOMME-MAIL:	
Scheduling Activity:	NMITC
SADSN:	433-0126
SACOMM:	(757) 433-0126
SADSNFAX:	N/A
SACOMMFAX:	N/A
SACOMME-MAIL:	
Reviewing Activity:	CNET

Title:	**CHEMICAL AND BIOLOGICAL WARFARE INTELLIGENCE COURSE (CABWIC)**
UJTL Reference:	ST.2; SN.2
Course Number:	N/A
Objective:	To know the capabilities of and threat posed by the use of CBW agents.
Description:	This is a basic introductory course designed for intelligence personnel who have had limited (if any) exposure to CBW training. It features experts on CBW from a variety of agencies whose mission includes the monitoring and countering of the CBW threat. Topics include: a survey of the concepts and principles of CBW; the foreign CBW threat; protection in the CBW environment; and CBW impact on military operations.
Audience:	Limited to intelligence professionals involved with threat projections and assessments, and intelligence personnel whose unit position is directly related to Chemical and Biological Warfare.
Clearance:	SECRET
Prerequisites:	NONE
Length:	5 days
Frequency:	2 classes per year
Capacity:	Varies
Location:	JMITC, Bolling AFB, MD
VTC:	NONE
Distance Learning:	NONE
Cost:	Per diem and travel to the training location.
Funding:	By parent organization
Curriculum Manager:	JMITC, DAJ-1
CMDSN:	428-2791
CMCOMM:	(202) 231-2791
CMDSNFAX:	428-8497
CMCOMMFAX:	(202) 231-8497
CMCOMME-MAIL:	
Scheduling Activity:	JMITC, DAJ-2C
SADSN:	428-3108
SACOMM:	(202) 231-3108
SADSNFAX:	428-2810
SACOMMFAX:	(202) 231-2810
SACOMME-MAIL:	
Reviewing Activity:	DIA/JMITC

Title:	**INDICATIONS AND WARNING COURSE (I&WC)**
UJTL Reference:	ST.2; SN.2
Course Number:	N/A
Objective:	To understand the fundamentals of indicator-based methodology, understand the principles of warning and warning systems, and to know existing problems, structures, and operations.
Description:	Principles of indications and warning, evolution of warning systems, Defense I&W System methodology, derivation of indicators, warning practical exercise, related collection support, Deception, joint intelligence centers, national intelligence support to regional crises, terrorism and narcotics as warning problems, and a field trip to the National Military Joint Intelligence Center (NMJIC).
Audience:	Primarily for watch officers/NCOs and analysts who support the warning functions in joint intelligence centers or other warning centers in the Defense Indications and Warning System or non-DOD counterparts. Others in I&W related activities are eligible and encouraged to attend on a space-available basis.
Clearance:	TOP SECRET
Prerequisites:	Working in the field of I&W.
Length:	2 weeks
Frequency:	2 classes per year
Capacity:	Varies
Location:	JMITC, Bolling AFB, MD
VTC:	NONE
Distance Learning:	NONE
Cost:	Per diem and travel to the training location.
Funding:	By parent organization
Curriculum Manager:	JMITC, DAJ-1
CMDSN:	428-2791
CMCOMM:	(202) 231-2791
CMDSNFAX:	428-8497
CMCOMMFAX:	(202) 231-8497
CMCOMME-MAIL:	
Scheduling Activity:	JMITC, DAJ-2C
SADSN:	428-3108
SACOMM:	(202) 231-3108
SADSNFAX:	428-2810
SACOMMFAX:	(202) 231-2810
SACOMME-MAIL:	
Reviewing Activity:	DIA/JMITC

Title:	**INDICATIONS AND WARNING SHORT COURSE (I&WSC)**
UJTL Reference:	ST.2; SN.2
Course Number:	N/A
Objective:	To understand the principles of warning and be able to demonstrate proficiency in the indicator-based methodology used by the Defense Indications and Warning System.
Description:	This course covers the principles of indications and warning, evolution of warning systems, Defense I&W System methodology, derivation of indicators, warning practices exercise, the warning responsibilities of joint intelligence centers, and national intelligence support to regional crises. Upon request, other topics such as Deception can be included.
Audience:	Government personnel who are assigned to, scheduled for assignment to, supported by, or receive support from warning intelligence activities.
Clearance:	TOP SECRET/SCI
Prerequisites:	Duties relate to I&W.
Length:	5/8-hour classes on weekends
Frequency:	As required
Capacity:	Varies
Location:	JMITC, Bolling AFB, MD
VTC:	NONE
Distance Learning:	NONE
Cost:	Per diem and travel to the training location.
Funding:	By parent organization
Curriculum Manager:	JMITC, DAJ-1
CMDSN:	428-4195
CMCOMM:	(202) 231-4195
CMDSNFAX:	428-8497
CMCOMMFAX:	(202)231-8497
CMCOMME-MAIL:	
Scheduling Activity:	JMITC, DAJ-2C
SADSN:	428-2797
SACOMM:	(202) 231-2797
SADSNFAX:	428-2810
SACOMMFAX:	(202) 231-2810
SACOMME-MAIL:	
Reviewing Activity:	DIA/JMITC

Title:	**MOBILE COLLECTION MANAGERS COURSE (M/CMC)**
UJTL Reference:	ST.2; SN.2
Course Number:	N/A
Objective:	To train DOD CRM personnel on specific aspects of the DOD CRM system and its processes and procedures, as identified by the requestor.
Description:	Collection Management (CM) and its components, CRM, and collection operations management (COM); interactive CM; sensor selection; the DOD CRM system; intelligence collection systems capabilities, limitations, and resources; CRM processes and procedures. Training will cover national, theater, and military Services intelligence collection systems in the IMINT, SIGINT, MASINT, and HUMINT disciplines; key organizations in the CRM system; how to perform sensor selection and interactive CM; and how to formulate and submit requirements as nominations for collection by discipline and time sensitivity.
Audience:	Limited to DOD military and civilian personnel of all grades who are assigned to CRM billets and whose duties require them to possess an in-depth knowledge of the DOD CRM system and its processes and procedures.
Clearance:	TOP SECRET/SI/TK
Prerequisites:	Students must be assigned to CRM billets of the Unified Commands and/or their Component Commands, and of other DOD Commands and Agencies that have a requirement to submit requirements for intelligence collection by DOD and national systems.
Length:	5 days
Frequency:	As required/requested
Capacity:	Varies
Location:	JMITC, Bolling AFB, MD
VTC:	NONE
Distance Learning:	MTT to requestor location
Cost:	TDY and per diem for instructors.
Funding:	Requestor/sponsor fund cites required NLT 30 days prior to MTT departure for CONUS and 45 days for OCONUS training requests.
Curriculum Manager:	JMITC, DAJ-1
CMDSN:	428-8661
CMCOMM:	(202) 231-8661
CMDSNFAX:	428-2753
CMCOMMFAX:	(202) 231-2753
CMCOMME-MAIL:	
Scheduling Activity:	JMITC, DAJ-1
SADSN:	428-3286
SACOMM:	(202) 231-3286
SADSNFAX:	428-2753
SACOMMFAX:	(202) 231-2753
SACOMME-MAIL:	
Reviewing Activity:	DIA/JMITC

Title:	**MOBILE COUNTERDRUG ANALYST COURSE (M/CDAC)**
UJTL Reference:	ST.2; SN.2
Course Number:	N/A
Objective:	This course enables comprehension of the nature of the organized criminal activity in narcotics trafficking, the process of analyzing these organizations, and equips each student with the necessary methodological tools to derive the requisite intelligence.
Description:	Discusses the current salient analytic issues in the counternarcotics arena, depiction of the elements of a narcotics trafficking organization and explanation of the intelligence cycle as it pertains to counterdrug analysis. This course can be given in different versions: it can be tailored to a DOD intelligence or Law Enforcement audience.
Audience:	Intelligence analyst with counterdrug duties.
Clearance:	UNCLASSIFIED
Prerequisites:	NONE
Length:	2-3 days
Frequency:	As requested
Capacity:	Minimum 20 students; maximum 35 students
Location:	JMITC, Bolling AFB, MD
VTC:	NONE
Distance Learning:	MTT to requesting organization location
Cost:	TDY and per diem for instructors.
Funding:	Requestor/sponsor fund cites required NLT 30 days prior to MTT departure for CONUS and 45 days for OCONUS training requests.
Curriculum Manager:	JMITC, DAJ-1
CMDSN:	428-3286
CMCOMM:	(202) 231-3286
CMDSNFAX:	428-2753
CMCOMMFAX:	(202) 231-2753
CMCOMME-MAIL:	
Scheduling Activity:	JMITC, DAJ-1
SADSN:	428-3286
SACOMM:	(202) 231-3286
SADSNFAX:	428-2753
SACOMMFAX:	(202) 231-2753
SACOMME-MAIL:	
Reviewing Activity:	DIA/JMITC

Title:	**MOBILE INDICATIONS AND WARNING (M/I&W)**
UJTL Reference:	ST.2; SN.2
Course Number:	N/A
Objective:	To understand the principles of warning and be able to demonstrate proficiency in the indicator-based methodology used by the Defense Indications and Warning System.
Description:	This course covers the principles of I&W, evolution of warning systems, Defense I&W System methodology, derivation of indicators, warning practical exercise, the warning responsibilities of joint intelligence centers, and national intelligence support to regional crises. Upon request, other topics such as Deception may be included.
Audience:	Primarily for military or civilian personnel who perform warning functions in joint intelligence centers or other warning centers, as well as personnel who support the I&W function.
Clearance:	TOP SECRET/SCI
Prerequisites:	NONE
Length:	5 days
Frequency:	As required/requested
Capacity:	Minimum 20 students; maximum 30 students
Location:	JMITC, Bolling AFB, MD
VTC:	NONE
Distance Learning:	MTT to requesting organization location
Cost:	TDY and per diem for instructors.
Funding:	Requestor/sponsor fund cites required NLT 30 days prior to MTT departure for CONUS and 45 days for OCONUS training requests.
Curriculum Manager:	JMITC, DAJ-1
CMDSN:	428-3286
CMCOMM:	(202) 231-3286
CMDSNFAX:	428-2753
CMCOMMFAX:	(202) 231-2753
CMCOMME-MAIL:	
Scheduling Activity:	JMITC, DAJ-1
SADSN:	428-3286
SACOMM:	(202) 231-3286
SADSNFAX:	428-2753
SACOMMFAX:	(202) 231-2753
SACOMME-MAIL:	
Reviewing Activity:	DIA/JMITC

Title:	**MOBILE MODERNIZED INTEGRATED DATA BASE (MIDB) 2.X FUNDAMENTALS AND APPLICATIONS (M/MIDBFA)**
UJTL Reference:	ST.2; SN.2
Course Number:	IIS021
Objective:	To understand the basic concepts and capabilities inherent to data retrieval and report production within the MIDB system and to perform basic retrieval and output procedures.
Description:	Provides instruction on the basic capabilities and functions of the MIDB 2.X as a tool to support analytical applications. It includes an overview of the MIDB 2.X file structure and data relationships. Provides emphasis on MIDB 2.X user interfaces, help functions, data manipulation, graphical capabilities, including the TMTK mapping function, and basic database production functions (NOM/DCR). This course serves as a prerequisite for the MIDB 2.X Production Courses.
Audience:	Intelligence analysts/technicians with need to use database.
Clearance:	TOP SECRET/SCI
Prerequisites:	Intelligence analyst training/experience, GUI knowledge.
Length:	4 days
Frequency:	As required/requested
Capacity:	Dependent upon availability of workstations
Location:	JMITC, Bolling AFB, MD
VTC:	NONE
Distance Learning:	MTT to requesting organization location
Cost:	TDY and per diem for instructors.
Funding:	Requestor/sponsor fund cite required NLT 30 days prior to MTT departure for CONUS and 45 days for OCONUS training requests.
Curriculum Manager:	JMITC, DAJ-1
CMDSN:	428-3286
CMCOMM:	(202) 231-3286
CMDSNFAX:	428-2753
CMCOMMFAX:	(202) 231-2753
CMCOMME-MAIL:	
Scheduling Activity:	JMITC, DAJ-05
SADSN:	428-3286
SACOMM:	(202) 231-3286
SADSNFAX:	428-2753
SACOMMFAX:	(202) 231-2753
SACOMME-MAIL:	
Reviewing Activity:	DIA/JMITC

Title:	**MOBILE MODERNIZED INTEGRATED DATA BASE PRODUCTION FOR UNITS (M/MIDBPU)**
UJTL Reference:	ST.2; SN.2
Course Number:	N/A
Objective:	To thoroughly understand the MIDB data content, its structure, and production rules in order to maintain the data base's currency and integrity.
Description:	This course provides General Military Intelligence Unit/Order of Battle production analysts instruction on the basic capabilities, functions and requirements necessary to adequately perform maintenance tasks on the Modernized Integrated Data Base (MIDB) units view and Unit related installation/facility view records. Students learn the essential system procedures required to keep the MIDB as current and accurate as possible. Emphasis is placed on learning the basic standard operation procedures/ requirements (SOP); the Shared Production Program; use of application and system support data bases; use of all help functions; and the NOM/DCR validations process.
Audience:	Primarily for military and civilian personnel who perform MIDB maintenance functions in joint intelligence centers.
Clearance:	TOP SECRET/SCI; No Contract Completion of MIDB
Prerequisites:	Fundamentals and Applications Course and MIDB production responsibility.
Length:	5 days
Frequency:	As required/requested
Capacity:	Dependent upon availability of terminals
Location:	JMITC, Bolling AFB, MD
VTC:	NONE
Distance Learning:	MTT to requesting organization location
Cost:	TDY and per diem for instructors.
Funding:	Requestor/sponsor fund cites required NLT 30 days prior to MTT departure for CONUS and 45 days for OCONUS training requests.
Curriculum Manager:	JMITC, DAJ-1
CMDSN:	428-3286
CMCOMM:	(202) 231-3286
CMDSNFAX:	428-2753
CMCOMMFAX:	(202) 231-2753
CMCOMME-MAIL:	
Scheduling Activity:	JMITC, DAJ-1
SADSN:	428-3286
SACOMM:	(202) 231-3286
SADSNFAX:	428-2753
SACOMMFAX:	(202) 231-2753
SACOMME-MAIL:	
Reviewing Activity:	DIA/JMITC

Title:	**MOBILE MODERNIZED INTEGRATED DATA BASE 2.X TRAIN-THE-TRAINER FOR USER TRANSITION COURSE (M/MIDBT3TR)**
UJTL Reference:	ST.2; SN.2
Course Number:	IIS025
Objective:	To apply appropriate teaching techniques and to demonstrate a mastery of the skills and knowledge of the MIDB 2.X system in order to effectively conduct the MIDB 2.X User Transition Course at the student trainer's command.
Description:	Provides certified MIDB 1.X T3 instructors with the skills and knowledge to instruct the MIDB 2.X User Transition Course to MIDB 2.X users. The course will emphasize the new features, differences between the MIDB 1.X and MIDB 2.X systems, instructional perspectives, instruction of practical exercises, and MIDB 2.X instructional problem areas.
Audience:	Potential MIDB 2.X trainers.
Clearance:	TOP SECRET/SCI
Prerequisites:	Current certified MIDB 1.X T3 trainer.
Length:	2 weeks
Frequency:	As required/requested
Capacity:	Dependent upon availability of workstations
Location:	JMITC, Bolling AFB, MD
VTC:	NONE
Distance Learning:	MTT to requesting organization location
Cost:	TDY and per diem for instructors.
Funding:	Requestor/sponsor fund cite required NLT 30 days prior to MTT departure for CONUS and 45 days for OCONUS training requests.
Curriculum Manager:	JMITC, DAJ-1
CMDSN:	428-3286
CMCOMM:	(202) 231-3286
CMDSNFAX:	428-2753
CMCOMMFAX:	(202) 231-2753
CMCOMME-MAIL:	
Scheduling Activity:	JMITC, DAJ-1
SADSN:	428-3286
SACOMM:	(202) 231-3286
SADSNFAX:	428-2753
SACOMMFAX:	(202) 231-2753
SACOMME-MAIL:	
Reviewing Activity:	DIA/JMITC

Title:	**MOBILE MODERNIZED INTEGRATED DATA BASE 2.X USER TRANSITION COURSE (M/MIDBUT)**
UJTL Reference:	ST.2; SN.2
Course Number:	IIS026
Objective:	To acquaint trained, experienced MIDB 1.X users with the new MIDB 2.X system.
Description:	Provides the trained MIDB 1.X user with instruction on the new MIDB 2.X system with emphasis on the syntax, user interfaces, data manipulation, NOM/DCR process, and data production features. The MIDB 2.X structure changes and naming conventions will also be stressed. In addition, this course gives a general presentation on the additional databases which have been added as extensions to the MIDB 2.X system.
Audience:	Intelligence analysts/technicians with need to use database.
Clearance:	TOP SECRET/SCI
Prerequisites:	MIDB 1.X trained.
Length:	4 days
Frequency:	As required/requested
Capacity:	Dependent upon availability of workstations
Location:	JMITC, Bolling AFB, MD
VTC:	NONE
Distance Learning:	MTT to requesting organization location
Cost:	TDY and per diem for instructors.
Funding:	Requestor/sponsor fund cite required NLT 30 days prior to MTT departure for CONUS and 45 days for OCONUS training requests.
Curriculum Manager:	JMITC, DAJ-1
CMDSN:	428-3286
CMCOMM:	(202) 231-3286
CMDSNFAX:	428-2753
CMCOMMFAX:	(202) 231-2753
CMCOMME-MAIL:	
Scheduling Activity:	JMITC, DAJ-1
SADSN:	428-3286
SACOMM:	(202) 231-3286
SADSNFAX:	428-2753
SACOMMFAX:	(202) 231-2753
SACOMME-MAIL:	
Reviewing Activity:	DIA/JMITC

Title:	**MOBILE MODERNIZED INTEGRATED DATA BASE 2.X TRAIN-THE-TRAINER (T3) FOR FUNDAMENTALS AND APPLICATIONS (M/MIDBT3FA)**
UJTL Reference:	ST.2; SN.2
Course Number:	IIS027
Objective:	To apply appropriate teaching techniques and to demonstrate a mastery of the skills and knowledge of the MIDB 2.X system in order to conduct the MIDB 2.X Fundamentals and Applications at the student trainer's command.
Description:	Provides candidate trainers with the skills and knowledge to teach MIDB 2.X Fundamentals and Applications. Conducted at sites specified by the customer, this program consists of a brief review of MIDB 2.X retrieval techniques, practical exercises using courseware, and participation in faculty development training. In addition, the candidate trainers experience presenting MIDB 2.) course lectures, conducting demonstrations and performing various MIDB 2.X exercises.
Audience:	Potential MIDB 2.X Fundamentals and Applications trainers.
Clearance:	TOP SECRET/SCI
Prerequisites:	Instructor training/experience, GUI knowledge.
Length:	2 weeks
Frequency:	As required/requested
Capacity:	Dependent upon availability of workstations
Location:	JMITC, Bolling AFB, MD
VTC:	NONE
Distance Learning:	MTT to requesting organization location
Cost:	TDY and per diem for instructors.
Funding:	Requestor/sponsor fund cite required NLT 30 days prior to MTT departure for CONUS and 45 days for OCONUS training requests.
Curriculum Manager:	JMITC, DAJ-1
CMDSN:	428-3286
CMCOMM:	(202) 231-3286
CMDSNFAX:	428-2753
CMCOMMFAX:	(202) 231-2753
CMCOMME-MAIL:	
Scheduling Activity:	JMITC, DAJ-1
SADSN:	428-3286
SACOMM:	(202) 231-3286
SADSNFAX:	428-2753
SACOMMFAX:	(202) 231-2753
SACOMME-MAIL:	
Reviewing Activity:	DIA/JMITC

Title:	**MOBILE MODERNIZED INTEGRATED DATA BASE 2.X MANAGER'S OVERVIEW COURSE (MIDBMO)**
UJTL Reference:	ST.2; SN.2
Course Number:	IIS120
Objective:	To understand new principles employed within the MIDB 2.X with emphasis on the MIDB 2.X utilization in site production responsibilities and its ability to support information retrieval, evaluation and exploitation as the primary intelligence provider.
Description:	Introduces managers and supervisors to the history of MIDB, their roles and responsibilities associated with MIDB 2.X, the Shared Production Program, and the MIDB 2.X structural design. It provides instruction on syntax, user interfaces, data manipulation, a short overview of data production features, and a demonstration of the TMTK mapping capabilities.
Audience:	Managers/supervisors of MIDB users/analysts/production analysts.
Clearance:	TOP SECRET/SCI
Prerequisites:	GUI knowledge.
Length:	One-half days
Frequency:	As required/requested
Capacity:	20
Location:	JMITC, Bolling AFB, MD
VTC:	NONE
Distance Learning:	NONE
Cost:	TDY and per diem to the training location.
Funding:	By parent organization
Curriculum Manager:	JMITC, DAJ-1
CMDSN:	428-3436
CMCOMM:	(202) 231-3436
CMDSNFAX:	428-4206
CMCOMMFAX:	(202) 231-4206
CMCOMME-MAIL:	
Scheduling Activity:	JMITC, DAJ-2C
SADSN:	428-5215
SACOMM:	(202) 231-5215
SADSNFAX:	428-2810
SACOMMFAX:	(202) 231-2810
SACOMME-MAIL:	
Reviewing Activity:	DIA/JMITC

Title:	**MOBILE MODERNIZED INTEGRATED DATA BASE 2.X FUNDAMENTALS AND APPLICATIONS (MIDBFA)**
UJTL Reference:	ST.2; SN.2
Course Number:	IIS121
Objective:	To understand the basic concepts and capabilities inherent to data retrieval and report production within the MIDB system and to perform basic retrieval and output procedures.
Description:	Provides instruction on the basic capabilities and functions of the MIDB 2.0 as a tool to support analytical applications. It includes an overview of the MIDB 2.0 file structure and data relationships. Provides emphasis on MIDB 2.0 user interfaces, help functions, data manipulation, graphical capabilities, including the TMTK mapping function, and basic database production functions (NOMDCR). This course serves as a prerequisite for the MIDB 2.0 Production Courses.
Audience:	Intelligence analysts/technicians with need to use database.
Clearance:	TOP SECRET/SCI
Prerequisites:	Intelligence analyst/training/experience, GUI knowledge.
Length:	4 days
Frequency:	10 times per year; additional courses as needed
Capacity:	16 or 20
Location:	JMITC, Bolling AFB, MD
VTC:	NONE
Distance Learning:	NONE
Cost:	TDY and per diem to the training location.
Funding:	By parent organization
Curriculum Manager:	JMITC, DAJ-1
CMDSN:	428-8654
CMCOMM:	(202) 231-8654
CMDSNFAX:	428-4206
CMCOMMFAX:	(202) 231-4206
CMCOMME-MAIL:	
Scheduling Activity:	JMITC, DAJ-2C
SADSN:	428-5215
SACOMM:	(202) 231-5215
SADSNFAX:	428-2810
SACOMMFAX:	(202) 231-2810
SACOMME-MAIL:	
Reviewing Activity:	DIA/JMITC

Title:	**MOBILE MODERNIZED INTEGRATED DATA BASE 2.X TRAIN-THE-TRAINER (T3) FOR FUNDAMENTALS AND APPLICATIONS (MIDBT3FA)**
UJTL Reference:	ST.2; SN.2
Course Number:	IIS124
Objective:	To apply appropriate teaching techniques and to demonstrate a mastery of the skills and knowledge of the MIDB 2.X system in order to conduct the MIDB 2.X Fundamentals and Applications at the student trainer's command.
Description:	Provides candidate trainers with the skills and knowledge to teach MIDB 2.X Fundamentals and Applications. Conducted at sites specified by the customer, this program consists of a brief review of MIDB 2.X retrieval techniques, practical exercises using courseware, and participation in faculty development training. In addition, the candidate trainers experience presenting MIDB 2.) course lectures, conducting demonstrations and performing various MIDB 2.X exercises.
Audience:	Potential MIDB 2.X Fundamentals and Applications trainers.
Clearance:	TOP SECRET/SCI
Prerequisites:	Instructor/training experience, GUI knowledge.
Length:	2 weeks
Frequency:	4 times per year
Capacity:	15 maximum
Location:	JMITC, Bolling AFB, MD
VTC:	NONE
Distance Learning:	NONE
Cost:	TDY and per diem to the training location.
Funding:	By parent organization
Curriculum Manager:	JMITC, DAJ-1
CMDSN:	428-8654
CMCOMM:	(202) 231-8654
CMDSNFAX:	428-4206
CMCOMMFAX:	(202) 231-4206
CMCOMME-MAIL:	
Scheduling Activity:	JMITC, DAJ-2C
SADSN:	428-5215
SACOMM:	(202) 231-5215
SADSNFAX:	428-2810
SACOMMFAX:	(202) 231-2810
SACOMME-MAIL:	
Reviewing Activity:	DIA/JMITC

Title:	**MOBILE MODERNIZED INTEGRATED DATA BASE 2.X TRAIN-THE-TRAINER FOR USER TRANSITION (MIDBT3TR)**
UJTL Reference:	ST.2; SN.2
Course Number:	IIS125
Objective:	To apply appropriate teaching techniques and to demonstrate a mastery of the skills and knowledge of the MIDB 2.X system in order to effectively conduct the MIDB 2.X User Transition Course at the student trainer's command.
Description:	Provides certified MIDB 1.X T3 instructors with the skills and knowledge to instruct the MIDB 2.X User Transition Course to MIDB 2.X users. The course will emphasize the new features, differences between the MIDB 1.X and MIDB 2.X systems, instructional perspectives, instruction of practical exercises, and MIDB 2.X instructional problem areas.
Audience:	Potential MIDB 2.X trainers.
Clearance:	TOP SECRET/SCI
Prerequisites:	Current certified MIDB 1.X T3 trainer.
Length:	2 weeks
Frequency:	As required/requested
Capacity:	15 maximum
Location:	JMITC, Bolling AFB, MD
VTC:	NONE
Distance Learning:	NONE
Cost:	TDY and per diem to the training location.
Funding:	By parent organization
Curriculum Manager:	JMITC, DAJ-1
CMDSN:	428-8654
CMCOMM:	(202) 231-8654
CMDSNFAX:	428-4206
CMCOMMFAX:	(202) 231-4206
CMCOMME-MAIL:	
Scheduling Activity:	JMITC, DAJ-2C
SADSN:	428-5215
SACOMM:	(202) 231-5215
SADSNFAX:	428-2810
SACOMMFAX:	(202) 231-2810
SACOMME-MAIL:	
Reviewing Activity:	DIA/JMITC

Title:	**MOBILE MODERNIZED INTEGRATED DATA BASE 2.X USER TRANSITION COURSE (MIDBUT)**
UJTL Reference:	ST.2; SN.2
Course Number:	IIS126
Objective:	To acquaint trained, experienced MIDB 1.X users with the new MIDB 2.X system.
Description:	Provides the trained MIDB 1.X user with instruction on the new MIDB 2.X system with emphasis on the syntax, user interfaces, data manipulation, NOM/DCR process, and data production features. The MIDB 2.X structure changes and naming conventions will also be stressed. In addition, this course gives a general presentation on the additional databases which have been added as extensions to the MIDB 2.X system.
Audience:	Intelligence analysts/technicians with need to use database.
Clearance:	TOP SECRET/SCI
Prerequisites:	MIDB 1.X trained.
Length:	4 days
Frequency:	As required/requested
Capacity:	16 or 20
Location:	JMITC, Bolling AFB, MD
VTC:	NONE
Distance Learning:	NONE
Cost:	TDY and per diem to the training location.
Funding:	By parent organization
Curriculum Manager:	JMITC, DAJ-1
CMDSN:	428-8654
CMCOMM:	(202) 231-8654
CMDSNFAX:	428-4206
CMCOMMFAX:	(202) 231-4206
CMCOMME-MAIL:	
Scheduling Activity:	JMITC, DAJ-2C
SADSN:	428-5215
SACOMM:	(202) 231-5215
SADSNFAX:	428-2810
SACOMMFAX:	(202) 231-2810
SACOMME-MAIL:	
Reviewing Activity:	DIA/JMITC

Title:	**MOBILE JOINT INTELLIGENCE ANALYST COURSE (M/JIAC)**
UJTL Reference:	ST.2; SN.2
Course Number:	N/A
Objective:	To provide a baseline of general and specialized knowledge and competencies in the different intelligence functions and analytic techniques to support skills needed in a joint national intelligence production environment.
Description:	Training will cover the National Foreign Intelligence Community; the analytic process and critical thinking; different analytic techniques; and the aspects of military capabilities analysis.
Audience:	Primarily for military or civilian personnel who perform intelligence analysis functions in joint intelligence centers.
Clearance:	TOP SECRET/SCI
Prerequisites:	Intelligence personnel from Unified Commands and other analytic support centers who are being assigned or are assigned analytical positions within the production facility.
Length:	5 days
Frequency:	As required/requested
Capacity:	JMITC, Bolling AFB, MD
Location:	Minimum 20 students; maximum 30 students
VTC:	NONE
Distance Learning:	MTT to requesting organization location
Cost:	TDY and per diem for the instructors.
Funding:	Requestor/sponsor fund cites required NLT 30 days prior to MTT departure for CONUS and 45 days for OCONUS training requests.
Curriculum Manager:	JMITC, DAJ-1
CMDSN:	428-3286
CMCOMM:	(202) 231-3286
CMDSNFAX:	428-2753
CMCOMMFAX:	(202) 231-2753
CMCOMME-MAIL:	
Scheduling Activity:	JMITC,DAJ-1
SADSN:	428-3286
SACOMM:	(202) 231-3286
SADSNFAX:	428-2753
SACOMMFAX:	(202) 231-2753
SACOMME-MAIL:	
Reviewing Activity:	DIA/JMITC

Title:	**MODERNIZED INTEGRATED DATABASES TRAIN-THE-TRAINER (T3) FOR FUNDAMENTALS AND APPLICATIONS (MIDBT37A)**
UJTL Reference:	ST.2; SN.2
Course Number:	N/A
Objective:	To understand and apply appropriate teaching techniques and to demonstrate a mastery of the skills and knowledge of the MIDB system in order to effectively conduct the MIDB Fundamentals and Applications.
Description:	Provides candidate trainers with the skills and knowledge to teach MIDB Fundamentals and Applications. The program consists of a brief review of the MIDB retrieval, techniques, practical exercises using courseware, participation in faculty development training, and experience presenting MIDB course lectures, demonstrations, and exercises.
Audience:	Intelligence analyst with computer experience.
Clearance:	TOP SECRET/SCI; No Contract
Prerequisites:	Completion of MIDB Fundamentals and Applications, intelligence experience, teaching/trainer experience, computer skills, and data base experience.
Length:	2 weeks
Frequency:	3 classes per year
Capacity:	Varies
Location:	JMITC, Bolling AFB, MD
VTC:	NONE
Distance Learning:	NONE
Cost:	Per diem and travel to the training location.
Funding:	By parent organization
Curriculum Manager:	JMITC, DAJ-1
CMDSN:	428-2791
CMCOMM:	(202) 231-2791
CMDSNFAX:	428-8497
CMCOMMFAX:	(202) 231-8497
CMCOMME-MAIL:	
Scheduling Activity:	JMITC, DAJ-2C
SADSN:	428-3108
SACOMM:	(202) 231-3108
SADSNFAX:	428-2810
SACOMMFAX:	(202) 231-2810
SACOMME-MAIL:	
Reviewing Activity:	DIA/JMITC

Title:	**MOBILE COUNTERTERRORISM ANALYSIS COURSE (M/CAC)**
UJTL Reference:	ST.2; SN.2, SN.3; ST.8
Course Number:	N/A
Objective:	To understand major issues confronting community counterterrorism analysts, the nature of the terrorist threat, and the tools and techniques for counterterrorism analysis.
Description:	This course is a mobile version of the entry-level resident course and includes: an overview of the Counterterrorism Community and extent of the terrorist threat; terrorist motivation and operations; terrorism indication and warning; analytical pointers/resources; association matrices/link analysis/visual investigative analysis; all day practical exercise; terrorism in the 1990s; and based on user need, a theater threat overview.
Audience:	Intelligence analysts with counterterrorist duties.
Clearance:	SECRET/NOFORN
Prerequisites:	Assigned to counterterrorist duties.
Length:	4 days
Frequency:	As requested
Capacity:	Minimum 20 students; maximum 30 students
Location:	JMITC, Bolling AFB, MD
VTC:	NONE
Distance Learning:	MTT to requestor location.
Cost:	TDY and per diem for instructors.
Funding:	Requestor/sponsor fund cites required NLT 30 days prior to MTT departure for CONUS and 45 days for OCONUS training requests.
Curriculum Manager:	JMITC, DAJ-1
CMDSN:	428-3286
CMCOMM:	(202) 231-3286
CMDSNFAX:	428-2753
CMCOMMFAX:	(202) 231-2753
CMCOMME-MAIL:	
Scheduling Activity:	JMITC, DAJ-1
SADSN:	428-3286
SACOMM:	(202) 231-3286
SADSNFAX:	428-2753
SACOMMFAX:	(202) 231-2753
SACOMME-MAIL:	
Reviewing Activity:	DIA/JMITC

Title:	**INTELLIGENCE ANALYST COURSE (IAC)**
UJTL Reference:	ST.2; SN.2
Course Number:	N/A
Objective:	To know the fundamentals of general intelligence analysis as preparation for assigned analytical duties.
Description:	This course provides an entry-level for newly-assigned general intelligence analysts at the national or strategic level. The analytic process and critical thinking; the role of analysts in the intelligence community, the components of strategic intelligence as structuring tools in an analytic problem; intelligence functions performed and the analyst's role in each segment of the intelligence cycle (requirements, validation, collection, analysis, production, dissemination, and evaluation). Emphasis is on the role of the intelligence analyst, research techniques, and various analytic techniques commonly used by analysts. Training includes lectures, analytical case studies, and practical exercise. Career status: This course is mandatory for entry level general intelligence personnel (DOD Manual 1430.1-M-3).
Audience:	Personnel in grades O-1 through O-4; E-5 through E-7; or GS-5 through GS-11 who are or will be associated with general intelligence analysis. Individuals of higher grade, who are being assigned for the first time in the intelligence or analysis fields, may request a waiver to the grade requirement. This course is mandatory for entry-level general intelligence personnel.
Clearance:	SECRET
Prerequisites:	A working knowledge of the US Intelligence Community, or successful completion of the National Intelligence Course (NIC).
Length:	2 weeks
Frequency:	5 classes per year
Capacity:	Varies
Location:	JMITC, Bolling AFB, MD
VTC:	NONE
Distance Learning:	NONE
Cost:	Per diem and travel to the training location.
Funding:	By parent organization
Curriculum Manager:	JMITC, DAJ-1
CMDSN:	428-3333
CMCOMM:	(202) 231-3333
CMDSNFAX:	428-8497
CMCOMMFAX:	(202) 231-8497
CMCOMME-MAIL:	
Scheduling Activity:	JMITC, DAJ-2C
SADSN:	428-2797
SACOMM:	(202) 231-2797
SADSNFAX:	428-2810
SACOMMFAX:	(202) 231-2810
SACOMME-MAIL:	
Reviewing Activity:	DIA/JMITC

Title:	**JOINT TARGETING STAFF COURSE**
UJTL Reference:	ST.2, ST.3; OP.2, OP.3
Course Number:	USN: S-3A-0005
	USAF: X50ZN14N3-014
	USA: ATRRS 303 JTS001
Objective:	Provide formal joint targeting training for mid-career operations and intelligence personnel destined for either: (1) designated joint targeting positions at the Unified Commands, the Joint Staff, and Defense Agencies; or (2) Service designated targeting positions which by their nature could be expected to be involved in joint targeting operations.
Description:	Three weeks (14 training days) of classroom oriented instruction, practical exercises, and labs.
Audience:	Operations and intelligence personnel: officers 0-3 to 0-5, enlisted E-5 to E-7, and civilians GS-11 to GS-15 working in or destined for joint targeting related positions at Joint Commands, Defense Agencies, and the Services.
Clearance:	SECRET NOFORN. Enhancement classes taught at TOP SECRET/SCI level for those with clearance.
Prerequisites:	NONE
Length:	3 weeks (14 training days)
Frequency:	8 classes per year
Capacity:	30 students per class
Location:	Dam Neck, VA
VTC:	Not available
Distance Learning:	Mobile Training Teams available to export portions of the course when classes are not in session.
Cost:	Per diem and travel to training location.
Funding:	By parent organization
Curriculum Manager:	JTS AOIC, FCTCL Dam Neck, Virginia Beach, VA
CMDSN:	433-0295
CMCOMM:	(757) 433-0295
CMDSNFAX:	433-0280
CMCOMMFAX:	(757) 433-0280
CMCOMME-MAIL:	
Scheduling Activity:	JTS Quota Control
SADSN:	433-0277
SACOMM:	(757) 433-0277
SADSNFAX:	433-0280
SACOMMFAX:	(757) 433-0280
SACOMME-MAIL:	
Reviewing Activity:	USJFCOM J-7

Title:	**JOINT TARGETING APPLICATIONS COURSE**
UJTL Reference:	ST.2, ST.3; OP.2, OP.3
Course Number:	USN: S-3A-0005
	USAF: X50ZN14N3-014
	USA: ATRRS 303 JTS001
Objective:	Provide formal joint weaponeering training and weapons employment consideration for mid-career operations and intelligence personnel destined for either: (1) designated joint targeting positions at the Unified Commands, the Joint Staff, and Defense Agencies; or (2) Service designated targeting positions which by their nature could be expected to be involved in joint targeting operations.
Description:	Two weeks (9 training days) of classroom oriented instruction and labs.
Audience:	Operations and intelligence personnel: officers 0-3 to 0-5, enlisted E-5 to E-7, and civilians GS-11 to GS-15 working in or destined for joint targeting related positions at Joint Commands, Defense Agencies, and the Services.
Clearance:	SECRET NOFORN
Prerequisites:	Completion of the Joint Targeting Staff Course is recommended but not required.
Length:	2 weeks (9 training days)
Frequency:	8 classes per year
Capacity:	30 students per class
Location:	Dam Neck, VA
VTC:	Not available
Distance Learning:	Not available
Cost:	Per diem and travel to training location.
Funding:	By parent organization
Curriculum Manager:	JTS AOIC, FCTCL Dam Neck, Virginia Beach, VA
CMDSN:	433-0295
CMCOMM:	(757) 433-0295
CMDSNFAX:	433-0280
CMCOMMFAX:	(757) 433-0280
CMCOMME-MAIL:	
Scheduling Activity:	JTS Quota Control
SADSN:	433-0277
SACOMM:	(757) 433-0277
SADSNFAX:	433-0280
SACOMMFAX:	(757) 433-0280
SACOMME-MAIL:	
Reviewing Activity:	USJFCOM J-7

Title:	**JOINT BATTLE DAMAGE ASSESSMENT COURSE**
UJTL Reference:	ST.2, ST.3; OP.2, OP.3
Course Number:	USN: S-3A-0005
	USAF: X50ZN14N3-014
	USA: ATRRS 303 JTS001
Objective:	Provide a detailed background in all aspects of the battle damage assessment process. Covers methodologies employed to accurately assess and communicate the effectiveness of weapons delivered against a variety of targets.
Description:	One week (5 training days) of classroom oriented instruction, practical exercises, and labs.
Audience:	Qualified operations and intelligence personnel: officers 0-1 to 0-5, enlisted E-5 to E-9, and civilians GS-9 to GS-14 working in or destined for Unified Commands, the Joint Staff, and Defense Agencies who are designated to augment the National Military Joint Intelligence Center (NMJIC), Theater JICs, Joint Task Forces (JTFs), or component BDA cells.
Clearance:	SECRET NOFORN
Prerequisites:	NONE
Length:	1 week (5 training days)
Frequency:	8 classes per year
Capacity:	30 students per class
Location:	Dam Neck, VA
VTC:	Not available
Distance Learning:	Mobile Training Teams available to export portions of the course when classes are not in session.
Cost:	Per diem and travel to training location.
Funding:	By parent organization
Curriculum Manager:	JTS AOIC, FCTCL Dam Neck, Virginia Beach, VA
CMDSN:	433-0295
CMCOMM:	(757) 433-0295
CMDSNFAX:	433-0280
CMCOMMFAX:	(757) 433-0280
CMCOMME-MAIL:	
Scheduling Activity:	JTS Quota Control
SADSN:	433-0277
SACOMM:	(757) 433-0277
SADSNFAX:	433-0280
SACOMMFAX:	(757) 433-0280
SACOMME-MAIL:	
Reviewing Activity:	USJFCOM J-7

Title:	**JOINT FORCES AIR COMPONENT COMMANDER (JFACC) COURSE**
UJTL Reference:	ST.3; OP.3, OP.6
Course Number:	N/A
Objective:	Understand current US doctrine for joint and combined operations and the role of the JFACC. Understand US Army, Navy, Air Force, and Marine Corps doctrinal concepts for theater warfare. Understand the integration of weapons systems and command and control systems from different Services to provide effective theater air defense and respond to differences of opinion among Services over theater air power employment concepts and the role of the JFACC. Be able to assist CINC/JTF development of military objectives, end states and the joint scheme of maneuver. Understand theater air strategy development to support the theater campaign. Be able to execute theater air strategy.
Description:	A senior military education course hosted by the US Air Force, sponsored by all four Services. Designed to prepare potential JFACCs for theater-level combat leadership responsibilities. The attendees study warfighting, military doctrine, and the application of unified, joint, and combined forces, with particular emphasis on air power employment in theater-level operations.
Audience:	Joint Service 0-7 officers (All Services).
Clearance:	TOP SECRET/SCI (SAP)
Prerequisites:	NONE
Length:	7 days
Frequency:	Semi-annually
Capacity:	17 attendees
Location:	Maxwell AFB, AL
VTC:	Capacity exists through Air Wargaming Institute capability; however, all presentations are held on-site.
Distance Learning:	NONE
Cost:	Per diem and travel to the training location.
Funding:	Each Service funds its own attendees
Curriculum Manager:	AETC (POC: COL Lughinbuhl)
CMDSN:	493-5101
CMCOMM:	(334) 953-5101
CMDSNFAX:	493-7639
CMCOMMFAX:	(334) 953-7639
CMCOMME-MAIL:	
Scheduling Activity:	AETC (POC: Ms. Ballance)
SADSN:	493-7969
SACOMM:	(334) 953-7969
SADSNFAX:	493-7639
SACOMMFAX:	(334) 953-7639
SACOMME-MAIL:	
Reviewing Activity:	N/A

Title:	**AIR VEHICLE FORCE APPLICATION SYSTEM (AFAS)**
UJTL Reference:	ST.3, ST.6
Course Number:	N/A
Objective:	Instruction on how to apply the AFAS system for aircraft and cruise missile planning purposes.
Description:	A combined lecture and laboratory class consisting of approximately 8 hours of lecture and 24 hours of hands-on laboratory sessions.
Audience:	War planning officers, 0-4 and above.
Clearance:	SECRET for Classroom; TOP SECRET for laboratory portion
Prerequisites:	NONE
Length:	4 days
Frequency:	Quarterly, with monthly sessions during summer
Capacity:	40 students per year, with up to 6 students per session
Location:	Offutt AFB, NE
VTC:	NONE
Distance Learning:	NONE
Cost:	Per diem and travel to the training location.
Funding:	By parent organization
Curriculum Manager:	USSTRATCOM (POC: Mr. Will Kroeger)
CMDSN:	271-3302
CMCOMM:	(402) 294-3302
CMDSNFAX:	271-1323
CMCOMMFAX:	(402) 294-1323
CMCOMME-MAIL:	
Scheduling Activity:	USSTRATCOM (POC: Mr. Will Kroeger)
SADSN:	271-5141
SACOMM:	(402) 294-5141
SADSNFAX:	N/A
SACOMMFAX:	N/A
SACOMME-MAIL:	
Reviewing Activity:	N/A

Title:	**TLAM STAFF STRIKE OFFICER COURSE (TSSOC)**
UJTL Reference:	ST.3; OP.3, OP.5; TA.3, TA.5
Course Number:	NONE
Objective:	Provide advanced Tomahawk training for individuals selected for an "approved" billet.
Description:	The final course in an advanced training continuum for high level program managers and operational command staffs. This course is designed to familiarize and indoctrinate the student in advanced technical, planning, and employment issues related to the Tomahawk weapons system. TSSOC includes in-depth briefs and discussions with CMSA TLAM mission planners, fleet strike officers, program managers, and firing units. Site visits include briefs and demonstrations at USCINCPAC Cruise Missile Support Activity, CINCPACFLT, COMNAVSUBPAC, and Shore Targeting Terminal Watch Center, and tours of a TLAM-capable submarine and surface combatant.
Audience:	NCA staffs, OPNAV managers, JCS staff planners, National Military Command Center Senior Watch Officers, Unified CINC staff, Numbered Fleet staffs.
Clearance:	TOP SECRET/SCI
Prerequisites:	TLAM Tactical Commander Course and TLAM Mission Distribution System Course.
Length:	5 days
Frequency:	As required
Capacity:	5 students per class
Location:	Pt Loma Naval Complex, San Diego, CA
VTC:	NONE
Distance Learning:	NONE
Cost:	Per diem and travel to the training location.
Funding:	By parent organization
Curriculum Manager:	Tactical Training Group, Pacific (POC: CDR Tollefson)
CMDSN:	553-8341
CMCOMM:	(619) 553-8341
CMDSNFAX:	553-4731
CMCOMMFAX:	(619) 553-4731
CMCOMME-MAIL:	tolle@cod.nosc.mil
Scheduling Activity:	Tactical Training Group, Pacific (POC: CDR Tollefson)
SADSN:	553-8341
SACOMM:	(619) 553-8341
SADSNFAX:	553-4731
SACOMMFAX:	(619) 553-4731
SACOMME-MAIL:	tolle@cod.nosc.mil
Reviewing Activity:	N/A

Title:	**TLAM TACTICAL COMMANDER COURSE (TTCC)**
UJTL Reference:	ST.3, ST.5; OP.3, OP.5
Course Number:	K-2G-3005
Objective:	To provide an overview of TLAM capabilities; understanding of targeting/weaponeering criterion; understanding of mission planning; and demonstrate C2 planning.
Description:	An interactive seminar format course combining classroom instruction, equipment demonstrations, and practical scenarios. Topics include overviews of missile variants, planning system, distribution system, targeting cycle, weaponeering, TLAM C2, TLAM Command Information, environmental support issues, Tomahawk Strike Commander duties, launch area coordinator duties, TLAM messages, and TLAM/TACAIR coordination issues.
Audience:	NCA staff, OPNAV managers, JCS staff planners, National Military Command Center Senior Watch Officers, Unified CINC staff, Numbered Fleet staffs, Numbered Air Force Operations Group Staff, Afloat Task Group Commanders, afloat planners, task group staffs, afloat unit commanders (DESRON/CVWING), afloat unit commander staffs, launch platform prospective commanding officers (O-6), and staff cruise missile assistants (FCCS/OSCS).
Clearance:	TOP SECRET
Prerequisites:	NONE
Length:	4 days
Frequency:	5 classes per year
Capacity:	20 students per class
Location:	Tactical Training Group, Pacific
VTC:	NONE
Distance Learning:	NONE
Cost:	Per diem and travel to the training location.
Funding:	By parent organization
Curriculum Manager:	Tactical Training Group, Pacific (POC: CDR Brayn Tollefson)
CMDSN:	553-9949
CMCOMM:	(619) 553-9949
CMDSNFAX:	553-4731
CMCOMMFAX:	(619) 553-4731
CMCOMME-MAIL:	SIPRNET (suwsyn@fctc.pac.navy.smil.mil)l
Scheduling Activity:	Tactical Training Group, Pacific (POC: Mr. Jamie Catto)
SADSN:	553-8341
SACOMM:	(619) 553-8341
SADSNFAX:	553-4731
SACOMMFAX:	(619) 553-4731
SACOMME-MAIL:	tolle@cod.nosc.mil
Reviewing Activity:	N/A

Title:	**DAISY FOR MANAGERS COURSE**
UJTL Reference:	ST.4
Course Number:	ALMC-DV
Objective:	To prepare Defense Reutilization and Marketing Program (DRMP) supervisors and managers to utilize DAISY to manage their particular function at their level of the DRMP.
Description:	Designed to teach current operating and access procedures for the computer-based accounting and management system--DAISY--through hands-on computer based learning that is directly linked to the Defense Reutilization and Marketing Office (DRMO) accounts of the student enrollees. Emphasis is placed on interpreting primary report extracts, effective research through available DAISY products, design of reports to meet needs, and managing workload based on available accounting data.
Audience:	Military or civilian personnel (including local national) assigned to or on orders for assignment to a reutilization and marketing organization where extensive knowledge of DAISY is required. The primary target audience includes DRMO Chiefs and other DRMO personnel in managerial or supervisory positions.
Clearance:	NONE
Prerequisites:	44-80 DRMS-I: An Introduction (correspondence course).
Length:	1 week
Frequency:	6 classes per year
Capacity:	30 students per class
Location:	ALMC, Ft. Lee, VA
VTC:	NONE
Distance Learning:	NONE
Cost:	Per diem and travel to the training location.
Funding:	By parent organization
Curriculum Manager:	ALMC (POC: Mr. Cessna)
CMDSN:	539-4315
CMCOMM:	N/A
CMDSNFAX:	539-4647
CMCOMMFAX:	N/A
CMCOMME-MAIL:	
Scheduling Activity:	ALMC (POC: Mr. Cessna)
SADSN:	539-4315
SACOMM:	N/A
SADSNFAX:	539-4647
SACOMMFAX:	N/A
SACOMME-MAIL:	
Reviewing Activity:	HQ, DLA, MMSC

Title:	**DEFENSE DEMILITARIZATION COURSE**
UJTL Reference:	ST.4
Course Number:	ALMC-BD
Objective:	Teaches DOD item managers and technical managers to perform their functions regarding the Demilitarization (DEMIL) program.
Description:	Covers the DEMIL program administration and responsibilities to include DEMIL code determination and assignment, processing and property management of DEMIL required items at the DOD activity, DEMIL challenge program, and Trade Security Controls.
Audience:	Mandatory for all DOD personnel responsible for the assignment or review of demilitarization codes and all DOD personnel responsible for the management, administration and/or oversight of any aspect of the DEMIL and/or Trade Security Controls Program.
Clearance:	NONE
Prerequisites:	NONE
Length:	1 week
Frequency:	23 classes per year
Capacity:	30 students per class
Location:	Resident and On-Site (at varying locations)
VTC:	In agreement with the proponent, this course is scheduled to be taught via the Satellite Education Network (as well as on-site) in the future.
Distance Learning:	NONE
Cost:	Per diem and travel to the training location.
Funding:	By parent organization
Curriculum Manager:	ALMC (POC: Mr. Mooring)
CMDSN:	539-0226
CMCOMM:	N/A
CMDSNFAX:	539-4647
CMCOMMFAX:	N/A
CMCOMME-MAIL:	
Scheduling Activity:	ALMC (POC: Mr. Mooring)
SADSN:	539-0226
SACOMM:	N/A
SADSNFAX:	539-4647
SACOMMFAX:	N/A
SACOMME-MAIL:	
Reviewing Activity:	HQ, DLA, MMSC

Title:	**DEFENSE REUTILIZATION AND MARKETING COURSE-BASIC**
UJTL Reference:	ST.4
Course Number:	8G-F1
Objective:	To prepare DOD personnel to perform the functions of the Defense Reutilization and Marketing Program (DRMP) including receipt, classification, storage, reutilization, marketing and ultimate disposal, and to carry out their responsibilities in regard to special concerns and included programs.
Description:	Presents the DRMP concepts with emphasis on the detailed mechanics of basic disposal operations to include its objectives, policies, and procedures involved in the reutilization, donation, sale, ultimate disposal, DEMIL and other special processing of DOD excess and surplus personal property.
Audience:	Military and civilian personnel (including local national) assigned to the DRMP, and others such as IG, auditors, and criminal investigators whose duties require an in-depth knowledge of disposal operations.
Clearance:	NONE
Prerequisites:	44-80 DRMS-I, An Introduction (Correspondence Course).
Length:	3 weeks (including 1 week read ahead)
Frequency:	5 classes per year
Capacity:	30 students per class
Location:	Resident and On-Site (at varying locations)
VTC:	NONE
Distance Learning:	NONE
Cost:	Per diem and travel to the training location.
Funding:	By parent organization
Curriculum Manager:	ALMC (POC: Mr. Cessna)
CMDSN:	539-4315
CMCOMM:	N/A
CMDSNFAX:	539-4647
CMCOMMFAX:	N/A
CMCOMME-MAIL:	
Scheduling Activity:	ALMC (POC: Mr. Cessna)
SADSN:	539-4315
SACOMM:	N/A
SADSNFAX:	539-4647
SACOMMFAX:	N/A
SACOMME-MAIL:	
Reviewing Activity:	HQ, DLA, MMSC

Title:	**DEFENSE REUTILIZATION AND MARKETING COURSE-MODIFIED**
UJTL Reference:	ST.4
Course Number:	ALMC-TB
Objective:	To prepare DOD personnel to interact with the Reutilization and Marketing Program including turning in and withdrawing excess personal property and to be in compliance with existing laws and regulations concerning interface with the DRMP in regards to special programs such as demilitarization, precious metals recovery and hazardous property processing.
Description:	Designed to provide DOD and other federal government personnel an insight into the Defense Reutilization and Marketing Program through interface with the DRMOs. Emphasis is placed on the DRMP as a source of supply and interrogating the system for assets prior to new procurement.
Audience:	Military (including reservists), IG, auditors, criminal investigators and civilian and contractor personnel whose duties require some basic or selected knowledge of the DOD Reutilization and Marketing Program.
Clearance:	NONE
Prerequisites:	NONE
Length:	1 to 5 days, tailored to the particular needs of the requestor
Frequency:	4 classes per year
Capacity:	30 students per class
Location:	Resident and On-Site (at varying locations)
VTC:	NONE
Distance Learning:	NONE
Cost:	Per diem and travel to the training location.
Funding:	By parent organization
Curriculum Manager:	ALMC (POC: Mr. Cessna)
CMDSN:	539-4315
CMCOMM:	N/A
CMDSNFAX:	539-4647
CMCOMMFAX:	N/A
CMCOMME-MAIL:	
Scheduling Activity:	ALMC (POC: Mr. Cessna)
SADSN:	539-4315
SACOMM:	N/A
SADSNFAX:	539-4647
SACOMMFAX:	N/A
SACOMME-MAIL:	
Reviewing Activity:	HQ, DLA, MMSC

Title:	**DEFENSE REUTILIZATION AND MARKETING PROPERTY ACCOUNTING COURSE**
UJTL Reference:	ST.4
Course Number:	ALMC-IC
Objective:	To prepare DOD Reutilization and Marketing personnel to perform the functions associated with the input transaction processing and utilize the output data of DAISY to manage the accountable record of the DRMO.
Description:	Through hands-on computer based learning, this course teaches the detailed mechanized reutilization and marketing property accounting system and relates that system to current operating procedures. Emphasis is given to code recognition and interpretation of computer printouts.
Audience:	Military or civilian personnel (including local national) assigned to or on orders for assignment to a reutilization and marketing organization employing DAISY.
Clearance:	NONE
Prerequisites:	44-80 DRMS-I: An Introduction (Correspondence Course).
Length:	2 weeks
Frequency:	5 classes per year
Capacity:	30 students per class
Location:	Resident and On-Site (at varying locations)
VTC:	NONE
Distance Learning:	NONE
Cost:	Per diem and travel to the training location.
Funding:	By parent organization
Curriculum Manager:	ALMC (POC: Mr. Cessna)
CMDSN:	539-4315
CMCOMM:	N/A
CMDSNFAX:	539-4647
CMCOMMFAX:	N/A
CMCOMME-MAIL:	
Scheduling Activity:	ALMC (POC: Mr. Cessna)
SADSN:	539-4315
SACOMM:	N/A
SADSNFAX:	539-4647
SACOMMFAX:	N/A
SACOMME-MAIL:	
Reviewing Activity:	HQ, DLA, MMSC

Title:	**DEFENSE REUTILIZATION AND MARKETING SYSTEM: AN INTRODUCTION**
UJTL Reference:	ST.4
Course Number:	44-80
Objective:	Designed to provide sufficient knowledge to DOD personnel to allow them to effectively interface with the Defense Reutilization and Marketing Program (DRMP).
Description:	Self-paced correspondence that provides an overview of the Defense Reutilization and Marketing Program. Emphasis is placed on program policy, objectives, organizational structure, and functions and procedures for obtaining the program objectives. Specific areas covered include general overviews of the turn-in and issue procedures and demilitarization, precious metals and hazardous property requirements for DOD excess, and surplus personal property.
Audience:	Any military or civilian personnel whose job requires an understanding, an appreciation, or interface with the Defense Reutilization and Marketing Program.
Clearance:	NONE
Prerequisites:	NONE
Length:	50 hours correspondence
Frequency:	N/A
Capacity:	N/A
Location:	Resident and On-Site (at varying locations)
VTC:	N/A
Distance Learning:	N/A
Cost:	NONE
Funding:	NONE
Curriculum Manager:	ALMC (POC: Mr. Cessna)
CMDSN:	539-4315
CMCOMM:	N/A
CMDSNFAX:	539-4647
CMCOMMFAX:	N/A
CMCOMME-MAIL:	
Scheduling Activity:	ALMC (POC: Mr. Cessna)
SADSN:	539-4315
SACOMM:	N/A
SADSNFAX:	539-4647
SACOMMFAX:	N/A
SACOMME-MAIL:	
Reviewing Activity:	HQ, DLA, MMSC

Title:	**JOINT MPF STAFF PLANNING**
UJTL Reference:	ST.4
Course Number:	M12L8Q1
Objective:	To prepare students to perform staff planning for Maritime Prepositioning Force (MPF) operations.
Description:	Students are introduced to terminology, organizational, and planning principles particular to planning and conducting MPF operations. Practical exercises concentrate on the detailed planning necessary for a student to conduct MPF operations.
Audience:	Officers and enlisted (E-6 and above) and equivalent civilian or licensed Merchant Marine personnel.
Clearance:	NONE
Prerequisites:	Restricted to audience listed above.
Length:	4 days
Frequency:	4 resident classes per year
Capacity:	40 per class
Location:	EWTGPAC, Coronado, CA
VTC:	NONE
Distance Learning:	MTT to requesting organization location.
Cost:	Per diem and travel to the training location.
Funding:	Funded by requesting Command or organization
Curriculum Manager:	CO, Expeditionary Warfare Training Group Pacific (EWTGPAC) (POC: Ms Rodriguez)
CMDSN:	577-3720
CMCOMM:	(619) 437-3720
CMDSNFAX:	577-3627
CMCOMMFAX:	(619) 437-3627
CMCOMME-MAIL:	
Scheduling Activity:	CO, Expeditionary Warfare Training Group Pacific (EWTGPAC) (POC: Ms Rodriguez)
SADSN:	577-3720
SACOMM:	(619) 437-3720
SADSNFAX:	577-3627
SACOMMFAX:	(619) 437-3627
SACOMME-MAIL:	
Reviewing Activity:	CG, MCCDC

Title:	**MORTUARY AFFAIRS OFFICER**
UJTL Reference:	ST.4
Course Number:	8B-SI4V
Objective:	To ensure a military and civilian force structure trained and capable of upholding Memorandum of Policy Number 16, which states that: "... the remains of all members of the Armed Forces of the United States will be returned for permanent disposition according to the direction of the person authorized to direct disposition (PADD)."
Description:	Prepares officers to plan, coordinate and supervise the care of deceased personnel and their personal effects (PE) in a theater of operations during major conflicts, operations other than war, and mass disasters. Students will become thoroughly familiar with the joint tactics, techniques, and procedures for mortuary affairs support across the full range of military operations. This course maximizes hands-on practical application of lectures and conferences conducted by personnel (all experts in their respective areas) during a four day practical exercise. Additionally, students receive firsthand experience with remains during the field trip to the Richmond, VA, Medical Examiner's Office.
Audience:	Open to all active and reserve component officers of all branches of Service and DOD civilians who hold positions requiring mortuary affairs knowledge.
Clearance:	NONE
Prerequisites:	Enrollees should presently hold or anticipate an assignment to a mortuary affairs position.
Length:	2 weeks
Frequency:	Course is conducted and scheduled in accordance with demand.
Capacity:	As required by demand
Location:	Ft. Lee, VA
VTC:	NONE
Distance Learning:	NONE
Cost:	Per diem and travel to the training location.
Funding:	By parent organization
Curriculum Manager:	Mortuary Affairs Center (POC: Mr. Bourlier)
CMDSN:	687-3831
CMCOMM:	(804) 734-3831
CMDSNFAX:	687-4758
CMCOMMFAX:	(804) 734-4758
CMCOMME-MAIL:	
Scheduling Activity:	Mortuary Affairs Center
SADSN:	687-5312
SACOMM:	(804) 734-5312
SADSNFAX:	687-4758
SACOMMFAX:	(804) 734-4758
SACOMME-MAIL:	
Reviewing Activity:	SACS

Title:	**JOINT MARITIME INFORMATION ELEMENT COURSE (JMIE)**
UJTL Reference:	ST.5, ST.8
Course Number:	J-830-3002
Objective:	Focus is primarily on end user productivity in acquiring, viewing, and disseminating relevant data as it relates to counternarcotics activity.
Description:	Provides lectures and practical exercises on topics which include database, communication application, and system administration.
Audience:	Federal employees, law enforcement agencies, and DOD personnel assigned to maritime analysis/JSS operators.
Clearance:	SECRET
Prerequisites:	NONE
Length:	5 days
Frequency:	8 classes per year
Capacity:	10 students per class
Location:	NMITC, Dam Neck, VA
VTC:	NONE
Distance Learning:	NONE
Cost:	Per diem and travel to the training location.
Funding:	By parent organization
Curriculum Manager:	NMITC (Lt. Shirer)
CMDSN:	433-0323
CMCOMM:	(804) 433-0323
CMDSNFAX:	433-0045
CMCOMMFAX:	(804) 433-0045
CMCOMME-MAIL:	
Scheduling Activity:	US Coast Guard
SADSN:	N/A
SACOMM:	(202) 267-6346
SADSNFAX:	N/A
SACOMMFAX:	N/A
SACOMME-MAIL:	
Reviewing Activity:	CNET

Title:	**JOINT INFORMATION WARFARE ORIENTATION COURSE (JIWOC)**
UJTL Reference:	ST.5; OP.5
Course Number:	S-00-3340
Objective:	To acquaint military personnel and US Government civilian equivalents with the fundamentals of Information Warfare (IW) strategy. Similar to the resident joint C2W course (S-00-3339), but more basic.
Description:	This nonresident course complements the resident course but is not a substitute. The course covers aspects of coordinating joint IW activities and programs at the unified commands, sub-unified commands, joint task forces, components, Department of Defense (DOD) organizations, and other government organizations.
Audience:	W-1 to O-6 (negotiable) and equivalent-level civilians preparing for duty as joint or combined IW staff officers or IW officers operating in a joint environment. The course also has application for those involved in planning, operations, targeting, operations security, deception, intelligence, and communications.
Clearance:	Normally SECRET but can be tailored to the clearance level of the audience (unclassified to TS/SI/TK).
Prerequisites:	NONE
Length:	Normally 4 days but can be tailored in length from 2 to 5 days to meet sponsoring organization requirements.
Frequency:	As requested by sponsoring organizations--based on instructor availability.
Capacity:	As determined by host organization (minimum 20 students).
Location:	N/A
VTC:	In development
Distance Learning:	MTT to requesting organization location.
Cost:	Per diem and travel to host organization location.
Funding:	By host organization
Curriculum Manager:	AFSC (POC: LTC Hubbard)
CMDSN:	565-6680/81/82
CMCOMM:	(757) 445-6680/81/82
CMDSNFAX:	564-6381
CMCOMMFAX:	(757) 444-6381
CMCOMME-MAIL:	
Scheduling Activity:	ACSC/JCIWS-IW
SADSN:	565-6680/81/82
SACOMM:	(757) 445-6680/81/82
SADSNFAX:	564-6381
SACOMMFAX:	(757) 444-6381
SACOMME-MAIL:	
Reviewing Activity:	N/A

Title:	**JOINT MEDICAL PLANNERS COURSE**
UJTL Reference:	ST.5
Course Number:	N/A
Objective:	To prepare joint medical planners so they may be capable of functioning at a joint or combined service command headquarters and be capable of preparing a complete OPLAN ANNEX Q, Medical Services.
Description:	Instruction is to be lecture and practical exercise. Automated tools such as JOPES Medical Planning Module, and the Logistics External Processor Medical (LPXMED) are used.
Audience:	Joint Medical Planners/04-05.
Clearance:	SECRET
Prerequisites:	Students must be in or enroute to a joint or combined medical service position.
Length:	15 days
Frequency:	4 classes per year
Capacity:	20 students per class
Location:	Bethesda Naval School of Medicine, Bethesda, MD
VTC:	NONE
Distance Learning:	NONE
Cost:	Per diem and travel to the training location.
Funding:	By parent organization
Curriculum Manager:	HSETC (POC: CDR Miller)
CMDSN:	295-1250
CMCOMM:	(301) 295-1250
CMDSNFAX:	295-2652
CMCOMMFAX:	(301) 295-2652
CMCOMME-MAIL:	
Scheduling Activity:	HSETC (POC: CDR Miller)
SADSN:	295-1250
SACOMM:	(301) 295-1250
SADSNFAX:	295-2652
SACOMMFAX:	(301) 295-2652
SACOMME-MAIL:	
Reviewing Activity:	N/A

Title:	**JOINT SPECIAL OPERATIONS STAFF OFFICER COURSE (JSOSOC)**
UJTL Reference:	ST.5
Course Number:	AFSOC 154002
Objective:	For each student to know the unique functions and interrelationships of a special operations staff.
Description:	Seminar with guest speakers as the leaders of each respective class. Major areas of instruction cover: (1) USSOCOM overview and mission activities; (2) USSOCOM Joint Staff; (3) USSOCOM Service components; (4) Service staffs; (5) Sub-unified Special Operations Commands; (6) Joint Staff (J-3: Special Operations Division, and J-3 Counternarcotics Division); (7) OASD/SO-LIC; (8) Intelligence support to Special operations; (9) Regional Orientations; and (10) A personal account.
Audience:	Military officers or civilian equivalent in the grade O-3 through O-5 who are currently assigned or enroute to a special operations staff or a position which routinely interacts with special operations staffs.
Clearance:	TOP SECRET
Prerequisites:	NONE
Length:	10 days
Frequency:	5 classes per year
Capacity:	28-30 students per class
Location:	Hurlburt Field, FL
VTC:	NONE
Distance Learning:	NONE
Cost:	Per diem and travel to the training location.
Funding:	By parent organization (limited school funding allows 11 funded quotas per class, normally for SOF).
Curriculum Manager:	USAFSOS (POC: Capt Smith)
CMDSN:	579-6452
CMCOMM:	(904) 884-6452
CMDSNFAX:	579-7989
CMCOMMFAX:	(904) 884-7989
CMCOMME-MAIL:	
Scheduling Activity:	USAFSOS (POC: Mrs. Weber)
SADSN:	579-4731
SACOMM:	(904) 884-4731
SADSNFAX:	579-4732
SACOMMFAX:	(904) 884-4732
SACOMME-MAIL:	
Reviewing Activity:	N/A

Title:	**JOINT VISUALLY INTEGRATED DISPLAY SYSTEM (JVIDS)**
UJTL Reference:	ST.5
Course Number:	J-243-2959
Objective:	Prepares law enforcement agency and DOD personnel assigned counterdrug intelligence fusion activities the skills to effectively operate JVIDS.
Description:	Provides lectures and practical exercise designed to reinforce system capabilities. Topics include basic system orientation, information management, plot control/ management, communications, and tactical decision aids.
Audience:	Joint/DOD and federal law enforcement agency personnel with little or no experience in counterdrug operations or system proficiency.
Clearance:	SECRET
Prerequisites:	NONE
Length:	5 days
Frequency:	8 classes per year
Capacity:	10 students per class
Location:	NMITC, Dam Neck, VA
VTC:	NONE
Distance Learning:	NONE
Cost:	Per diem and travel to the training location.
Funding:	By parent organization
Curriculum Manager:	NMITC (Mr. McGary)
CMDSN:	433-0112
CMCOMM:	(757) 433-0112
CMDSNFAX:	433-0045
CMCOMMFAX:	(757) 433-0045
CMCOMME-MAIL:	
Scheduling Activity:	NMITC
SADSN:	433-0126
SACOMM:	(757) 433-0126
SADSNFAX:	N/A
SACOMMFAX:	N/A
SACOMME-MAIL:	
Reviewing Activity:	CNET

Title:	**JOINT SPECIAL OPERATIONS FORCES PRE-COMMAND COURSE**
UJTL Reference:	ST.5
Course Number:	2E-F95/011-F65
Objective:	To foster interoperability and develop cohesion among SOF Service Commanders.
Description:	Understanding of Joint and Service Special Operations doctrine, organizations, capabilities; provide new and refresher training in selected Special Operations functions and duties; teach principles and techniques of training management and leader development; provide insight into principles and procedures of interagency operations; explain the role of the Joint Force Special Operations Command Component, and the role of the Joint Chiefs of Staff in Special Operations and policy issues; to provide senior SOF leader insights and perspectives into SOF imperatives, trends, policies, and issues.
Audience:	SOF Command designees, or incumbent and SOF Command Senior Enlisted Advisor, or Command Sergeant Major, O-4 (P) through O-7 or E-9.
Clearance:	SECRET
Prerequisites:	Must be an active or reserve component current commander or command designee. Enlisted must be a Command Sergeant Major or Senior Enlisted Advisor. Selected individuals from intergovernmental agencies may also attend with J-1 USSOCOM approval.
Length:	5 days
Frequency:	2 classes per year
Capacity:	Varies
Location:	Ft. Bragg, NC
VTC:	NONE
Distance Learning:	NONE
Cost:	Per diem and travel to the training location.
Funding:	Service funded
Curriculum Manager:	USAJFKSWCS (POC: Mr. Williams)
CMDSN:	239-6616
CMCOMM:	(910) 432-6616
CMDSNFAX:	239-8302
CMCOMMFAX:	(910) 432-8302
CMCOMME-MAIL:	
Scheduling Activity:	USAJFKSWCS (POC: Mr. Williams)
SADSN:	239-6616
SACOMM:	(910) 432-6616
SADSNFAX:	239-8302
SACOMMFAX:	(910) 432-8302
SACOMME-MAIL:	
Reviewing Activity:	Joint SOF Institute, Education and Research Directorate (DSN 239-1084, Fax 239-5467)

Title:	**JOINT COMMAND AND CONTROL WARFARE ORIENTATION COURSE (JC2WOC)**
UJTL Reference:	ST.5; OP.5
Course Number:	S-00-3337
Objective:	To prepare US officers and civilian equivalents for duty as joint or combined C2W Staff Officers or Service C2W Officers operating in a joint environment.
Description:	A 2-3 day Orientation Course is offered to Unified Commands, Components and Services at the site of their choice, and can be tailored to the specific needs of the host command. The instruction emphasizes intelligence support to C2W, C2W philosophy and doctrine, C2W elements, and the C2W planning process. The primary method of instruction is lecture with discussion.
Audience:	US officers and civilian equivalents preparing for duty as joint or combined C2W Staff Officers or Service C2W Officers operating in a joint environment. The course also has applications for those in other positions such as operations, communications, intelligence and planning.
Clearance:	SECRET/NOFORN
Prerequisites:	NONE
Length:	2-3 days
Frequency:	As requested by sponsoring commands, based on instructor availability.
Capacity:	As determined by sponsoring organization.
Location:	AFSC, Norfolk, VA
VTC:	In development
Distance Learning:	MTT to requesting organization location.
Cost:	Per diem and travel to the requesting organization location.
Funding:	AFSC provides travel funds to Joint Organizations. Component/Single Service Orientation Course funds (travel costs for instructors) must be provided by the host organization.
Curriculum Manager:	AFSC (POC: LTC Peterson)
CMDSN:	565-6680
CMCOMM:	(757) 444-6680
CMDSNFAX:	564-6381
CMCOMMFAX:	(757) 444-6381
CMCOMME-MAIL:	
Scheduling Activity:	AFSC (POC: LTC Peterson)
SADSN:	565-6680
SACOMM:	(757) 444-6680
SADSNFAX:	564-6381
SACOMMFAX:	(757) 444-6381
SACOMME-MAIL:	
Reviewing Activity:	N/A

Title:	**JOINT INFORMATION WARFARE STAFF AND OPERATIONS COURSE (JIWSOC)**
UJTL Reference:	ST.5; OP.5
Course Number:	S-00-3339
Objective:	To educate military personnel and US Government civilian equivalents in Information Operations (IO) with a primary emphasis on Information Warfare (IW).
Description:	The course acquaints students with the offensive and defensive IW concepts employed at unified commands, sub-unified commands, joint task forces, components, Department of Defense (DOD) organizations, and other government organizations. The curriculum covers the emerging strategy of Information Operations with emphasis on terminology, doctrine, tactics, equipment, organizations, and joint planning that supports IO/IW. The presentations are primarily informal lectures with discussions. The course is augmented by guest lecturers and culminates with students applying IW strategy to a real-world exercise scenario.
Audience:	W-1 to O-6 and equivalent-level civilians preparing for duty as joint or combined IW staff officers or Service IW officers operating in a joint environment. The course is relevant for those serving in IO/IW cells and staff positions in operations, intelligence, and planning. **Note:** When requesting a quota, the following information is required: rank/rating, full name, SSN, work address, phone number, statement that you have a TS/SI/TK clearance, job assignment, and a brief statement as to need for the course.
Clearance:	TOP SECRET/SI/TK
Prerequisites:	NONE
Length:	2 weeks
Frequency:	6 classes per year
Capacity:	24 students per class
Location:	AFSC, Norfolk, VA
VTC:	In development
Distance Learning:	NONE
Cost:	Per diem and travel to the training location.
Funding:	By parent organization
Curriculum Manager:	AFSC (POC: LTC Hubbard)
CMDSN:	565-6680/81/82
CMCOMM:	(757) 445-6680/81/82
CMDSNFAX:	564-6381
CMCOMMFAX:	(757) 444-6381
CMCOMME-MAIL:	
Scheduling Activity:	AFSC/JCIWS-IW
SADSN:	565-6680/81/82
SACOMM:	(757) 445-6680/81/82
SADSNFAX:	564-6381
SACOMMFAX:	(757) 444-6381
CMCOMME-MAIL:	
Reviewing Activity:	N/A

Title:	**COLLEGE OF NAVAL WARFARE**
UJTL Reference:	ST.5; OP.5; SN.5
Course Number:	S-00-1101
Objective:	To enhance the professional capabilities of senior military officers and government agency civilians to make sound decisions in command, staff, and management positions in naval, joint, and combined environments, to provide them with a sound understanding of military strategy and operational art and instill in them joint attitudes and perspectives.
Description:	Conducted at graduate level using multidisciplinary study, small group seminars, lectures, simulation, and gaming. Divided into three major study areas: Strategy and Policy; National Security Decision Making; and Joint Military Operations.
Audience:	Military service members O-5 to O-6, equivalent civilians of government agencies.
Clearance:	TOP SECRET
Prerequisites:	Bachelor's Degree, Service selection board.
Length:	44 weeks for August start (smaller number of students starting in November or March are on station 51 weeks).
Frequency:	1 per year
Capacity:	195-225 students per session
Location:	Newport, RI
VTC:	NONE
Distance Learning:	NONE
Cost:	Permanent change of station (PCS) orders.
Funding:	By Service organization
Curriculum Manager:	Naval War College (POC: Mr. Calhoun)
CMDSN:	N/A
CMCOMM:	(401) 841-2245
CMDSNFAX:	N/A
CMCOMMFAX:	(401) 841-1297
CMCOMME-MAIL:	
Scheduling Activity:	Naval War College (POC: Mrs. Estabrooks)
SADSN:	N/A
SACOMM:	(401) 841-3598
SADSNFAX:	N/A
SACOMMFAX:	(401) 841-1297
SACOMME-MAIL:	
Reviewing Activity:	N/A

Title:	**COLLEGE OF CONTINUING EDUCATION SATELLITE NONRESIDENT SEMINARS AND CORRESPONDENCE PROGRAMS**
UJTL Reference:	ST.5; OP.5; SN.5
Course Number:	N/A
Objective:	To enhance the professional capabilities of military officers and government agency civilians to make sound decisions in command, staff, and management positions in naval, joint and combined environments, to provide them with a sound understanding of military strategy and operational art and instill in them joint attitudes and perspectives.
Description:	Conducted at the graduate level using multidisciplinary study, small group seminars and lectures. The curriculum parallels that of the resident College of Naval Command and Staff, using two modes of instruction: the Nonresident Seminar, conducted at specific sites through-out the US; and core courses: the Correspondence Course Program, offered worldwide. Divided into three core courses: Strategy and Policy (S&P); National Security Decision Making (NSDM); and Joint Maritime Operations (JMO). See website at http://www.usnwc.edu/nwc/cce/index.htm
Audience:	Seminar Program: O-3 and above, active duty and reserve component personnel of all services, and DOD GS-11 and above. Correspondence Program: Sea-service officers, on active duty, O-3 and above; O-4 and above for Naval Reservists and non-sea-service personnel; and DOD employees, GS-11 and above. On a limited basis, officers of other nations allied with the US may be enrolled in the Correspondence Program via the US Defense Attache Office or other US military agency office in their country. **Note:** The Chairman, Joint Chiefs of Staff has certified each of the Naval War College nonresident programs as an intermediate level (Command and Staff) school for Joint Professional Military Education, Phase I credit. This credit is extended to all Navy and Marine Corps personnel. However, acceptance of Phase I credit by other services varies. Prospective students from other than the Navy or Marine Corps should check on the individual service policy before enrolling. Effective with nonresident enrollments on 1 March 1984 and subsequent, the New England Association of Schools and Colleges, Inc. has accredited the Naval War College. This accreditation extends to the College of Continuing Education for purposes of granting a Degree in National Security and Strategy Studies is **not granted to nonresident students.**
Clearance:	SECRET for a section of JMO in the Nonresident Seminar.
Prerequisites:	Bachelor's degree and Naval War College, College of Continuing Education screening and acceptance.

Length:	Nonresident Seminar: Each core course is 32 weeks of instruction from September to April. Correspondence Course Program: S&P contains 5 modules; and JMO contains 6 modules. Each module takes approximately 60 days. Course can be completed in 18-24 months.
Frequency:	Sequencing of core courses varies with each satellite Nonresident Seminar site. Correspondence Course Program may begin upon acceptance into the program.
Capacity:	Total student load for the three core courses in the Nonresident Seminars is approximately 1000 students; the Correspondence Course Program is approximately 500 students.
Location:	N/A
VTC:	NONE
Distance Learning:	Seminar Program taught by adjunct faculty at selected locations throughout the US. Correspondence Program administered by resident College of Continuing Education faculty at the Naval War College.
Cost:	None to students.
Funding:	Cost of materials and faculty salary borne by NWC/ appropriate Seminar Program host commands/agencies.
Curriculum Manager:	Naval War College (POC: CAPT J. E. Jackson, USN, SC)
CMDSN:	948-6515
CMCOMM:	(401) 841-6515
CMDSNFAX:	948-2457
CMCOMMFAX:	(401) 841-2457
CMCOMME-MAIL:	jacksonj@usnwc.edu
Scheduling Activity:	College of Continuing Education, NWC
SADSN:	948-2135
SACOMM:	(401) 841-2135
SADSNFAX:	948-2457
SACOMMFAX:	(401) 841-2457
SACOMME-MAIL:	ccenrs@usnwc.edu
Reviewing Activity:	N/A

Title:	**COLLEGE OF NAVAL COMMAND AND STAFF**
UJTL Reference:	ST.5; OP.5; SN.5
Course Number:	S-00-1201
Objective:	To enhance the professional capabilities of mid-grade military officers and government agency civilians to make sound decisions in command, staff, and management positions in naval, joint, and combined environments, to provide them with a sound understanding of military strategy and operational art and instill in them joint attitudes and perspectives.
Description:	Conducted at graduate level using multidisciplinary study, small group seminars, lectures, simulation, and gaming. Divided into three major study areas: Strategy and Policy; National Security Decision Making; and Joint Maritime Operations.
Audience:	Military service members O-4 (or selected to O-4), equivalent civilians of government agencies.
Clearance:	TOP SECRET
Prerequisites:	Bachelor's Degree, Service selection board.
Length:	44 weeks for August start (smaller number of students starting in November or March are on station 51 weeks).
Frequency:	1 per year
Capacity:	255-265 students per session
Location:	Newport, RI
VTC:	NONE
Distance Learning:	NONE
Cost:	Permanent change of station (PCS) orders.
Funding:	By Service
Curriculum Manager:	Naval War College (POC: Mr. Calhoun)
CMDSN:	N/A
CMCOMM:	(401) 841-2245
CMDSNFAX:	N/A
CMCOMMFAX:	(401) 841-1297
CMCOMME-MAIL:	
Scheduling Activity:	Naval War College (POC: Mrs. Estabrooks)
SADSN:	N/A
SACOMM:	(401) 841-3598
SADSNFAX:	N/A
SACOMMFAX:	(401) 841-1297
SACOMME-MAIL:	
Reviewing Activity:	N/A

Title:	**JOINT PLANNING ORIENTATION COURSE (JPOC)**
UJTL Reference:	ST.5; OP.5; SN.1
Course Number:	N/A
Objective:	For each student to gain familiarity with the commands and agencies involved and the procedures and techniques used during deliberate and time-sensitive planning, using Joint Operation Planning and Execution System (JOPES). AFSC Pub 1 (The Joint Staff Officers Guide) is the primary reference and is provided to all students attending.
Description:	Students are introduced to the joint planning process that in peacetime is called deliberate planning, and in emergencies or crises, time-sensitive planning. Students are acquainted with the process of developing a contingency plan based on a CJCS task assignment, and the process used by the Joint Planning and Execution Community (JPEC) to develop timely recommendations to aid the NCA in making decisions involving US military force. Included is a discussion on the relationship between the National Security Strategy (NSS); Joint Strategic Planning System (JSPS); PPBS and JOPES. Organization and command relationships and the historical evolution are presented along with DOD's current combatant command structure. The course includes a discussion on major programs and initiatives to correct existing deficiencies and improves the joint planning and execution process. TRAINING FORMAT: The 16 lessons are presented in seminar for audiences large and small, limited only by classroom facilities, using 35MM slide, overhead VGTs, and video presentation.
Audience:	Primarily for personnel involved with planning and executing contingency plans assigned to the combatant command, their components, and subordinate commands, the Joint Staff, and Defense Agencies and Organizations reporting to the CJCS. Specialty and grade varies from E-5 (occasionally) through 0-6/GS-12/13. The target audience is action officers at the 0-4/0-5 level and civilian equivalents.
Clearance:	NONE
Prerequisites:	NONE
Length:	3 days (20 hours)
Frequency:	Twice annually at each of the Combatant Commands; four times annually in the Washington, D.C. area; and five times annually at the AFSC on weekends.
Capacity:	Approximately 4,000 students per year
Location:	Various locations
VTC:	NONE
Distance Learning:	MTT to requesting organization location.
Cost:	Per diem and travel for the Mobile Training Team.
Funding:	CJCS taskings are funded by AFSC. All other requests must be funded by the requesting organization.

Curriculum Manager:	AFSC (POC: LTC Antis; Ms. DeGeere; Mr. Rowse)
CMDSN:	564-5386
CMCOMM:	(757) 444-5386
CMDSNFAX:	564-5317
CMCOMMFAX:	(757) 444-5317
CMCOMME-MAIL:	
Scheduling Activity:	AFSC (POC: Ms. DeGeere; Mr. Rowse)
SADSN:	564-5386
SACOMM:	(757) 444-5386
SADSNFAX:	564-5317
SACOMMFAX:	(757) 444-5317
SACOMME-MAIL:	
Reviewing Activity:	N/A

Title:	**CONTINGENCY WARTIME PLANNING COURSE**
UJTL Reference:	ST.5; SN.5
Course Number:	MCADRE002
Objective:	Professional continuing education course that teaches Air Force war planners the basics of joint and Air Force war planning and force sustainment.
Description:	Curriculum consists of five blocks of instruction covering the following: national strategy, organization for national security, command relationships, strategic mobility, Joint Strategic Planning System (JSPS), JOPES, PPBS, computer systems for planning, COMPES, Air Force doctrine, JSCP, USAF War and Mobilization Plan, USAF Operational Planning Process, Designed Operational Capability and Status of Resources and Training System, aerospace roles and missions, mobilization, commander's mission options, the art of war, base level deployment, base support planning, plans security, the War Reserve Materiel Program, and Crisis Action Procedures. Sixty percent of the course is presented by lecture, supported by seminar, practical exercises and discussion.
Audience:	Contingency planners and functional managers in grades E-4 through 0-5, and their civilian equivalents.
Clearance:	SECRET
Prerequisites:	NONE
Length:	14 days
Frequency:	9 classes per year
Capacity:	72 students per class
Location:	Maxwell AFB, AL
VTC:	NONE
Distance Learning:	NONE
Cost:	Per diem and travel to the training location.
Funding:	463 Air Force quotas are Air University funded. All others are by parent organization.
Curriculum Manager:	AETC (POC: Lt Col Wheeler)
CMDSN:	493-2551
CMCOMM:	(334) 953-2551
CMDSNFAX:	493-4336
CMCOMMFAX:	(334) 953-4336
CMCOMME-MAIL:	
Scheduling Activity:	AETC (POC: Mr. Hill)
SADSN:	493-2638
SACOMM:	(334) 953-2638
SADSNFAX:	493-4336
SACOMMFAX:	(334) 953-4336
SACOMME-MAIL:	
Reviewing Activity:	AF-XOXW

Title:	**JOINT FLAG OFFICER WARFIGHTING COURSE (JFOWC)**
UJTL Reference:	ST.5; SN.5; OP.5
Course Number:	MAAFNJ007
Objective:	Understand the operational level of war and associated decision-making. Understand complexities of joint/ combined operations. Review challenges of employment from Component/JTF/Theater Commander level.
Description:	The JFOWC is the senior military education course in the department of defense, owned and controlled by the four Service Chiefs. The course prepares Service Chief-selected two-star officers of all four services for theater-level combat leadership responsibilities. The attendees study warfighting, military doctrine, and application of unified, joint, and combined combat forces so they will be better prepared to face future crises.
Audience:	0-8 officers from all services.
Clearance:	TOP SECRET/SCI
Prerequisites:	NONE
Length:	13 days
Frequency:	Semi-annually
Capacity:	18 attendees per class
Location:	Maxwell AFB, AL
VTC:	Capacity exists through Air Force Wargaming Institute capability; however, all presentations are held on-site.
Distance Learning:	NONE
Cost:	Per diem and travel to the training location.
Funding:	Each Service funds its own attendees
Curriculum Manager:	AETC (POC: Lt Col Luginbuhl)
CMDSN:	493-5101
CMCOMM:	(334) 953-5101
CMDSNFAX:	493-7639
CMCOMMFAX:	(334) 953-7639
CMCOMME-MAIL:	
Scheduling Activity:	AETC (POC: Ms. Urquhart)
SADSN:	493-5101
SACOMM:	(334) 953-5101
SADSNFAX:	493-7639
SACOMMFAX:	(334) 953-7639
SACOMME-MAIL:	
Reviewing Activity:	N/A

Title:	**JOINT COUNTERINTELLIGENCE STAFF OFFICERS**
UJTL Reference:	**COURSE (JCISOC)**
Course Number:	ST.6; SN.3
Objective:	N/A
Description:	To educate personnel directly supporting joint military operations on joint structure, crisis action planning, the four elements of CI (collection, analysis and production, investigations, and operations), staffing CI support to OPLANS, and the unique aspects of organizing and managing a joint CI Staff.
Audience:	Designed to build upon basic CI courses and practical experience. It outlines how CI contributes to military planning and operations at the national, combatant command, and joint task force levels. Emphasis is placed on successful integration of CI personnel and equipment into joint exercise, plans, and operations. Officers and senior NCOs E-6 to O-9 or civilian equivalent. Limited to US government personnel nominated by their agency or Service, currently assigned as or pending assignment to joint CI positions, or assigned to Service CI positions supporting joint military operations.
Clearance:	TOP SECRET/SCI
Prerequisites:	Assignment to CI positions supporting joint military operations.
Length:	1 week
Frequency:	3 classes per year
Capacity:	Varies
Location:	JMITC, Bolling AFB, MD
VTC:	NONE
Distance Learning:	NONE
Cost:	Per diem and travel to the training location.
Funding:	By parent organization
Curriculum Manager:	DIA/DAC-1B
CMDSN:	224-9157
CMCOMM:	(703) 614-9157
CMDSNFAX:	N/A
CMCOMMFAX:	N/A
CMCOMME-MAIL:	
Scheduling Activity:	JMITC, DAJ-2C
SADSN:	428-3108
SACOMM:	(202) 231-3108
SADSNFAX:	428-2810
SACOMMFAX:	(202) 231-2810
SACOMME-MAIL:	
Reviewing Activity:	DIA/JMITC

Title:	**SCI ADMINISTRATION COURSE (SCI-ADMIN)**
UJTL Reference:	ST.6; SN.3
Course Number:	N/A
Objective:	To know the regular SCI administrative procedures accomplished at DOD Special Security Offices.
Description:	Detailed instruction in every area of SCI administrative security procedures including personnel security, billet management, clearance passing procedures, indoctrination/debriefing procedures, security education, information security, classification, document control, courier procedures, and handling of security violations.
Audience:	E-4 to E-7 or GS-4 to GS-7. Skills training for specific functions. Presentation is tailored for persons new to special security work.
Clearance:	TOP SECRET/SI/TK
Prerequisites:	Must be assigned to or pending assignment to an SSO or other SCI security post in the Defense Special Security System.
Length:	1 week
Frequency:	8 classes per year
Capacity:	Varies
Location:	JMITC, Bolling AFB, MD
VTC:	NONE
Distance Learning:	NONE
Cost:	Per diem and travel to the training location.
Funding:	By parent organization
Curriculum Manager:	JMITC, DAJ-1
CMDSN:	428-2791
CMCOMM:	(202) 231-2791
CMDSNFAX:	428-8497
CMCOMMFAX:	(202) 231-8497
CMCOMME-MAIL:	
Scheduling Activity:	JMITC, DAJ-2C
SADSN:	428-3108
SACOMM:	(202) 231-3108
SADSNFAX:	428-2810
SACOMMFAX:	(202) 231-2810
SACOMME-MAIL:	
Reviewing Activity:	DIA/JMITC

Title:	**SCI CONTROL OFFICER'S COURSE (SCI-SSO)**
UJTL Reference:	ST.6; SN.3
Course Number:	N/A
Objective:	To know how to perform all the functions of an SSO in DOD and to be effective security advocates and advisors in their commands.
Description:	Overview of the origins and development of the SSO system, the Intelligence Community and security in DOD, the Defense Special Security System structure and relationships, the hostile threat to security, SSO operations and responsibilities, security of the SCI communications and computer data, personnel security standards and SCI eligibility determination, billet management, the SSO's role in personnel and information security, and issues affecting SCI security.
Audience:	Presentation is tailored for persons new to SSO responsibilities. Military officers O-1 to O-6; enlisted ranks E-7 to E-9; and civilians in grades GS-7 and above.
Clearance:	TOP SECRET/SI/TK
Prerequisites:	Must be assigned as or pending assignment as a Sensitive Compartmented Information (SCI) Control Officer (Special Security Officer -SSO), Alternate SSO, or other official with similar SCI security responsibilities in the Defense Special Security System.
Length:	8 days
Frequency:	6 classes per year
Capacity:	Varies
Location:	JMITC, Bolling AFB, MD
VTC:	NONE
Distance Learning:	NONE
Cost:	Per diem and travel to the training location.
Funding:	By parent organization
Curriculum Manager:	JMITC, DAJ-1
CMDSN:	428-2791
CMCOMM:	(202) 231-2791
CMDSNFAX:	428-8497
CMCOMMFAX:	(202) 231-8497
CMCOMME-MAIL:	
Scheduling Activity:	JMITC, DAJ-2C
SADSN:	428-3108
SACOMM:	(202) 231-3108
SADSNFAX:	428-2810
SACOMMFAX:	(202) 373-2810
SACOMME-MAIL:	
Reviewing Activity:	DIA/JMITC

Title:	**JOINT PSYCHOLOGICAL OPERATIONS COURSE (JPOC)**
UJTL Reference:	ST.3, ST.8; OP.3
Course Number:	AFSOC 143502
Objective:	For each student to appreciate and comprehend basic doctrine, organization, techniques, equipment, and capabilities of psychological operations in support of US national objectives throughout the spectrum of conflict. Focuses on specified geographical areas of military/political concerns.
Description:	The course is divided into three instructional areas: (1) Introduction to Psychological Operations, (2) Psychological Organization Policy Assets, (3) Case Studies & PSYOP Issues.
Audience:	E-5 to O-5 or civilian equivalent who need to have a working knowledge of PSYOP.
Clearance:	SECRET
Prerequisites:	Personnel serving in positions that require an awareness of psychological operations.
Length:	4 1/2 days
Frequency:	4 classes per year
Capacity:	Up to 90 students per class
Location:	Hurlburt Field, FL
VTC:	NONE
Distance Learning:	NONE
Cost:	Per diem and travel to the training location.
Funding:	By parent organization
Curriculum Manager:	USAFSOS (POC: CAPT Rowlett)
CMDSN:	579-6908
CMCOMM:	(904) 884-6908
CMDSNFAX:	579-7989
CMCOMMFAX:	(904) 884-7989
CMCOMME-MAIL:	
Scheduling Activity:	USAFSOS (POC: Mrs. Weber)
SADSN:	579-4731
SACOMM:	(904) 884-4731
SADSNFAX:	579-4732
SACOMMFAX:	(904) 884-4732
SACOMME-MAIL:	
Reviewing Activity:	N/A

Title:	**JOINT PSYCHOLOGICAL OPERATIONS STAFF PLANNING COURSE**
UJTL Reference:	ST.3, ST.8; OP.3
Course Number:	3A-F53/243-F12
Objective:	Provide selected US government agency personnel with the planning skills required to use joint and Service PSYOP doctrine and assets in the preparation and supervision of PSYOP in support of joint operations in peacetime, crisis, and open hostilities.
Description:	Psychological Operations; PSYOP Techniques and Procedures; Joint Planning; End-of-Course Exercise.
Audience:	O-4 and above; E-7 and above; GS-11 and above; Department of Defense, other US Government agency personnel, with approval of the Joint Staff J-33; International personnel with appropriate security clearance assigned to positions which require knowledge of PSYOP planning skills in support of joint/combined operations, officers O-3 and above; GS-09 and above; WO1-WO5 and E-6 and above are encouraged to attend.
Clearance:	SECRET
Prerequisites:	Personnel assigned to positions which require PSYOP planning skills in support of joint/combined operations.
Length:	2 weeks
Frequency:	4 classes per year
Capacity:	20 students per class
Location:	Ft. Bragg, NC
VTC:	NONE
Distance Learning:	NONE
Cost:	Per diem and travel to the training location (JFK Special Warfare Center, Ft. Bragg, NC).
Funding:	By parent organization
Curriculum Manager:	JSOFI
CMDSN:	239-7509
CMCOMM:	(910) 432-7509
CMDSNFAX:	239-5396
CMCOMMFAX:	(910) 432-5396
CMCOMME-MAIL:	
Scheduling Activity:	JSOFI
SADSN:	239-7509
SACOMM:	(910) 432-3676
SADSNFAX:	239-5866
SACOMMFAX:	(910) 432-5866
SACOMME-MAIL:	
Reviewing Activity:	N/A

Title:	**JOINT SENIOR PSYCHOLOGICAL OPERATIONS COURSE (JSPOC)**
UJTL Reference:	ST.3, ST.8; OP.3
Course Number:	AFSOC 150002
Objective:	For each student to comprehend the concepts of PSYOP and appreciate its contribution to US military operations and foreign policy.
Description:	Provides selected senior officers and civilians with an awareness of PSYOP and its contributions to US national objectives throughout the conflict environment.
Audience:	O-6 and above or civilian equivalent.
Clearance:	TOP SECRET
Prerequisites:	Duties requiring an awareness of PSYOP.
Length:	2 1/2 days
Frequency:	2 classes per year
Capacity:	20 students per class
Location:	Hurlburt Field, FL
VTC:	NONE
Distance Learning:	NONE
Cost:	Per diem and travel to the training location.
Funding:	Course is funded by USAFSOS
Curriculum Manager:	USAFSOS (POC: MAJ Messelheiser)
CMDSN:	579-1845
CMCOMM:	(904) 884-1845
CMDSNFAX:	579-7989
CMCOMMFAX:	(904) 884-7989
CMCOMME-MAIL:	
Scheduling Activity:	USAFSOS (POC: Mrs. Weber)
SADSN:	579-4731
SACOMM:	(904) 884-4731
SADSNFAX:	579-4732
SACOMMFAX:	(904) 884-4732
SACOMME-MAIL:	
Reviewing Activity:	N/A

Title:	**NATO STAFF OFFICER ORIENTATION COURSE (NSOOC)**
UJTL Reference:	ST.8
Course Number:	N/A
Objective:	NSOOC is specifically designed for US field grade officers enroute to their initial NATO staff assignment. The objective of the course is to enable the officer to become immediately effective in the NATO staff environment. The student becomes conversant with the NATO treaty and international cooperation; NATO terminology; command organization and functions; political, economic, and intercultural aspects of the Alliance; and international staff work.
Description:	NSOOC is a two-week orientation program conducted at the NDU. The course has a two-phased approach. The first phase consists of intensive instruction in the following subject areas: History of the Alliance; The Washington Treaty; NATO Headquarters Organization; Allied Command Atlantic Organization; Allied Command Europe Organization; Concept of Maritime Operations; Logistics and Standardization; Infrastructure; Defense Planning; Strategic Concept; The NATO Staff Environment. The second phase of NSOOC features a wide array of guest speakers, including representatives from the Joint Staff, OSD, State Department, the Intelligence Community, Capitol Hill, NATO Attaches, and Senior Flag and General Officers with current or recent NATO experience.
Audience:	All US field grade officers enroute to their initial NATO assignment will first attend the NATO Staff Officer Orientation Course. US officers going to national assignments that have an involvement in NATO or a need to understand NATO international security concerns are strongly recommended to attend the course. This course is also open to select federal employees and reserve component officers IAW grade requirements.
Clearance:	SECRET
Prerequisites:	NONE
Length:	2 weeks
Frequency:	7 classes per year
Capacity:	40 students per class
Location:	Ft. McNair, Washington DC
VTC:	NONE
Distance Learning:	Specialized NATO tutorials and presentations are available on video-tape for senior officials or agencies within the Washington, D.C. area or elsewhere as separately arranged with the course director.
Cost:	Per diem and travel to the training location.
Funding:	By parent organization

Curriculum Manager:	NDU (POC: Mr. Chalmer)
CMDSN:	325-3830
CMCOMM:	(202) 685-3830
CMDSNFAX:	325-3829
CMCOMMFAX:	(202) 685-3829
CMCOMME-MAIL:	
Scheduling Activity:	NDU (POC: YN2 Butts)
SADSN:	325-3828
SACOMM:	(202) 685-3828
SADSNFAX:	325-3829
SACOMMFAX:	(202) 685-3829
SACOMME-MAIL:	
Reviewing Activity:	N/A

Title:	**STRATEGIC DEPLOYMENT PLANNING COURSE (STRADPC)**
UJTL Reference:	OP.1
Course Number:	8C-F16/553/F-3
Objective:	Teach the strategic deployment planning process through seminar discussions, lectures, and exercises.
Description:	The STRADPC is designed for movement planners from the battalion/brigade levels to the Corps and Installation levels that focuses on strategic deployment planning. Students learn the concepts and key factors involved in deliberate and crisis action planning, as well as the organizational structure for joint planning. They discuss the requirements and capabilities of the strategic mobility triad and support operations at POEs and PODs. They are provided an overview of JOPES, TC ACCIS, and MOBCON. They also learn the essentials of mobilization and deployment. Throughout the course, students participate in a variety of deployment planning exercises.
Audience:	Personnel from all services, active and reserve components. 0-3 and above; WO2 and above; E-7 and above; GS-9 and above.
Clearance:	NONE
Prerequisites:	NONE
Length:	2 weeks
Frequency:	6 classes per year
Capacity:	22 students per class
Location:	Ft. Eustis, VA
VTC:	Limited
Distance Learning:	MTT to requesting organization location.
Cost:	Per diem and travel to the training location.
Funding:	By parent organization
Curriculum Manager:	USA Transportation Center and School (POC: CPT McCormick)
CMDSN:	927-2039
CMCOMM:	(757) 878-2039
CMDSNFAX:	927-4900
CMCOMMFAX:	(757) 878-4900
CMCOMME-MAIL:	
Scheduling Activity:	ATRRS
SADSN:	927-2039
SACOMM:	(757) 878-2039
SADSNFAX:	927-4900
SACOMMFAX:	(757) 878-4900
SACOMME-MAIL:	
Reviewing Activity:	N/A

Title:	**UNIT MOVEMENT OFFICER DEPLOYMENT PLANNING COURSE (UMODPC)**
UJTL Reference:	OP.1
Course Number:	8C-F17/353-F5
Objective:	Teach unit movement officer responsibilities through seminar discussions, lectures, and practical exercises.
Description:	Designed for personnel who are appointed to or under consideration for appointment to a unit/staff movement position involving unit deployments. It is structured to cover the responsibilities of unit movement personnel; deployment planning; unit movement plans; AUEL; preparation of unit supplies and equipment; blocking, bracing, packing, crating and tiedown procedures; rail movement; unit deployment through a seaport; theater reception; and redeployment.
Audience:	Personnel from all Services, active and reserve components. Commissioned Officers, Warrant Officers, Enlisted Personnel (E-5 and above), and DOD civilians.
Clearance:	NONE
Prerequisites:	NONE
Length:	2 weeks
Frequency:	10 classes per year
Capacity:	30 students per class
Location:	Ft. Eustis, VA
VTC:	Limited
Distance Learning:	MTT to requesting organization location.
Cost:	Per diem and travel to the training location.
Funding:	By parent organization
Curriculum Manager:	USA Transportation Center and School (POC: CPT Giovino)
CMDSN:	927-1575
CMCOMM:	(757) 878-1575
CMDSNFAX:	927-4900
CMCOMMFAX:	(757) 878-4900
CMCOMME-MAIL:	
Scheduling Activity:	ATRRS
SADSN:	927-2039
SACOMM:	(757) 878-2039
SADSNFAX:	927-4900
SACOMMFAX:	(757) 878-4900
SACOMME-MAIL:	
Reviewing Activity:	SACS

Title:	**AIR OPERATIONS CENTER SPACE APPLICATIONS COURSE (ASAC)**
UJTL Reference:	OP.3, OP.6
Course Number:	N/A
Objective:	Provides training on the effective exploitation and combat application of DOD, Civil, Commercial, and National space systems to Numbered Air Force HQ personnel in an Air Operations Center context.
Description:	The course emphasizes applications of space capabilities at the Joint Air Force Component Commander level. The course includes blocks of instruction on space system capabilities and their applications within the air tasking order cycle and an optional block on US national systems.
Audience:	Numbered Air Force HQ personnel.
Clearance:	SECRET--TOP SECRET/SCI
Prerequisites:	NONE
Length:	1.5 training days
Frequency:	11 times per year
Capacity:	Dependent upon hosting unit capacity
Location:	Numbered Air Force locations and Falcon AFB, CO
VTC:	NONE
Distance Learning:	NONE
Cost:	Per diem and travel to the training location.
Funding:	By parent organization
Curriculum Manager:	SWC/DOT (POC: Capt Bystroff)
CMDSN:	560-8348
CMCOMM:	(719) 567-8348
CMDSNFAX:	560-9591
CMCOMMFAX:	(719) 567-9591
CMCOMME-MAIL:	bystroffjr@fafb.af.mil
Scheduling Activity:	SWC/DOT Registrars
SADSN:	560-9649/8610/9645
SACOMM:	(719) 567-9640/8610/9645
SADSNFAX:	560-9591
SACOMMFAX:	(719) 567-9591
SACOMME-MAIL:	registr@fafb.af.mil
Reviewing Activity:	N/A

Title:	**JOINT TASK FORCE INTELLIGENCE MANAGER'S COURSE (JTF INTL MGR)**
UJTL Reference:	OP.2
Course Number:	J-3A-1955
Objective:	Prepares senior intelligence personnel to support the theater CINC's two-tiered warfighting strategy.
Description:	Provides instruction on joint principles, JTF organization and intelligence operations, national and Service component intelligence support, collection, dissemination, targeting, communications, and systems to support JTF intelligence operations.
Audience:	Available to all officer and enlisted intelligence personnel 0-3 to 0-6 and E-7 to E-9.
Clearance:	TOP SECRET/SCI
Prerequisites:	NONE
Length:	12 days
Frequency:	FITCPAC 4 classes per year. NMITC 6 classes per year.
Capacity:	FITCPAC 25 students per class. NMITC 25 students per class.
Location:	NMITC
VTC:	NONE
Distance Learning:	NONE
Cost:	Per diem and travel to the training location.
Funding:	By parent organization
Curriculum Manager:	NMITC
CMDSN:	433-8014
CMCOMM:	(757) 433-8014
CMDSNFAX:	433-8210
CMCOMMFAX:	(757) 433-8210
CMCOMME-MAIL:	
Scheduling Activity:	NMITC
SADSN:	433-8097
SACOMM:	(757) 433-8097
SADSNFAX:	N/A
SACOMMFAX:	N/A
SACOMME-MAIL:	
Reviewing Activity:	CNET

Title:	**INTELLIGENCE COLLECTION MANAGERS COURSE (ICMC)**
UJTL Reference:	OP.2; ST.2; SN.2
Course Number:	N/A
Objective:	To train DOD personnel assigned to Collection Requirements Management (CRM) billets in the processes and procedures of the DOD CRM system.
Description:	Collection Management (CM) and its components, CRM, and Collection Operations Management (COM); interactive CM; sensor selection; the DOD CRM system; intelligence collection systems capabilities, limitations, and resources; CRM processes and procedures. Training will cover national, theater, and Military Services intelligence collection systems in the IMINT, SIGINT, MASINT, and HUMINT disciplines; key organizations in the CRM system; how to perform sensor selection and interactive CM; and how to formulate and submit requirements as nominations for collection by discipline and time sensitivity. The course will culminate in a practical exercise in which the students, acting as the CRM element of a Joint Task Force (JTF) will take the JTF commander's intelligence information requirements and turn them into nominations for collection by IMINT, HUMINT, SIGINT, and MASINT.
Audience:	Limited to DOD military and civilian personnel of all grades who are assigned to or enroute to CRM billets within the DOD.
Clearance:	TOP SECRET/SCI
Prerequisites:	Students must be assigned to or enroute to Collection Requirements Managers billets within the DOD, and must not have attended ICMC previously.
Length:	3 weeks
Frequency:	5 classes per year
Capacity:	Varies
Location:	JMITC, Bolling AFB, MD
VTC:	NONE
Distance Learning:	NONE
Cost:	Per diem and travel to the training location.
Funding:	By parent organization
Curriculum Manager:	JMITC, DAJ-1
CMDSN:	243-2791
CMCOMM:	(202) 373-2791
CMDSNFAX:	243-8497
CMCOMMFAX:	(202) 373-8497
CMCOMME-MAIL:	
Scheduling Activity:	JMITC, DAJ-2C
SADSN:	243-3108
SACOMM:	(202) 373-3108
SADSNFAX:	243-2810
SACOMMFAX:	(202) 373-2810
SACOMME-MAIL:	
Reviewing Activity:	DIA/JMITC

Title:	**INTRODUCTION TO INFORMATION OPERATIONS (IIO)**
UJTL Reference:	OP.2; OP.6
Course Number:	N/A
Objective:	To enhance students' background and understanding of the nature, evolving concepts, and implications of information warfare including: salient aspects of the information age, the revolution in military affairs, offensive and defensive aspects of information-based warfare, and implications of information-based warfare for the field of intelligence.
Description:	Students will read background material assigned by the course director and attend lectures and panels to include presentations by invited experts from the Defense Department and the private sector as well as allied nations. Extensive dialogue with dynamic speakers.
Audience:	Personnel in the civilian grade GS, SM or GG 11-15; military personnel in the grades of O-3 to O-6.
Clearance:	TOP SECRET
Prerequisites:	NONE
Length:	1 week
Frequency:	As required
Capacity:	36 students per class
Location:	JMITC, Bolling AFB, MD
VTC:	NONE
Distance Learning:	NONE
Cost:	Per diem and travel to the training location.
Funding:	By parent organization
Curriculum Manager:	JMITC, DAJ-1
CMDSN:	428-2296
CMCOMM:	(202) 231-3290
CMDSNFAX:	428-2797
CMCOMMFAX:	(202) 231-2797
CMCOMME-MAIL:	
Scheduling Activity:	JMITC, DAJ-1
SADSN:	428-2797
SACOMM:	(202) 231-2797
SADSNFAX:	428-2810
SACOMMFAX:	N/A
SACOMME-MAIL:	
Reviewing Activity:	JMITC

Title:	**JOINT AIR OPERATIONS SENIOR STAFF COURSE (JSSC)**
UJTL Reference:	SN.5; ST.5; OP.5; TA.5
Course Number:	N/A
Objective:	To understand the Joint Forces Air Component Commander (JFACC) organization, strategy development and typical equipment involved with the operations of a Joint Air Operations Center (JAOC). To understand how Contingency Theater Automated Planning System (CTAPS) and other related equipment are used to plan, produce, publish, disseminate, and execute an Air Tasking Order (ATO) and Airspace Control Order (ACO). To understand the Army, Navy, Air Force, and Marine Corps considerations and how they expect to function in a JAOC for the purpose of executing theater air operations. Examine additional current equipment which would be added to the theater battle management systems to aid the JFACC in accomplishing assigned responsibilities.
Description:	The JSSC is a senior professional military training program conducted at Hurlburt Field. The course uses presentations, discussions, and physical equipment to provide an overview of air operations strategy in joint operations. The program is designed to prepare attendees for senior leadership responsibilities in a JAOC. The program consists of senior speakers from many different areas of responsibility. Presentations by a General Officer JFACC and current Directors from different JAOC locations will lead off the program, followed by each services' operating considerations in a JAOC, and finishing with specific briefings and computer tools used in the JAOC.
Audience:	Joint Service 0-6 Officers.
Clearance:	Top Secret SCI
Prerequisites:	There are no prerequisites. The attendees are selected by their respective Numbered Air Force or equivalent organization based on potential for assignment as directors in a JAOC.
Length:	3.5 days
Frequency:	Semi-annually
Capacity:	18 attendees
Location:	Hurlburt Field, FL
VTC:	None
Distance Learning:	None
Cost:	Per diem and travel to the training location.
Funding:	By parent organization

Curriculum Manager:	USAFBTS/DJT (Mr. Shanks)
CMDSN:	579-6518
CMCOMM:	(850) 884-6518
CMDSNFAX:	579-5550
CMCOMMFAX:	(850) 884-5550
CMCOMME-MAIL:	shanks.robin@jfacc.hurlburt.af.mil
Scheduling Activity:	USAFBTS/DJT (Mr. Shanks)
SADSN:	579-6518
SACOMM:	(850) 884-6518
SADSNFAX:	579-5550
SACOMMFAX:	(850) 884-5550
SACOMME-MAIL:	shanks.robin@jfacc.hurlburt.af.mil
Reviewing Activity:	USAFBTS

Title:	**JOINT FORCE AIR COMPONENT COMMANDER (JFACC) GENERAL INFORMATION COURSE**
UJTL Reference:	OP.3, OP.5, OP.6
Course Number:	N/A
Objective:	Upon completion of the course, designated officers will possess the knowledge necessary to support a JFACC and contribute to the successful planning and execution of joint air operations.
Description:	This course is a self-study, self-paced instructional programmed text in CD-ROM format. This electronic version supercedes the earlier hard copy version dated Jun 96. It has been updated to more accurately reflect current and approved joint and Service doctrine and joint tactics, techniques, and procedures. Text from applicable approved joint publications (or Service publications when appropriate joint publications do not exist) is compiled in this single source and presented in a logical fashion. The course introduces joint task force staff officers and potential joint air operations center (JAOC) augmentees to the operation, roles, and responsibilities of a JFACC and the JAOC, and explains their contribution to the joint force mission.
Audience:	O-3 to O-6, identified JTF, JFACC, and JAOC staff members and augmentees.
Clearance:	N/A
Prerequisites:	N/A
Length:	Approximately 10 hours
Frequency:	N/A
Capacity:	N/A
Location:	N/A
VTC:	None
Distance Learning:	Download and CD-ROM order request information available at http://www.jwfc.js.mil/pages/courses.htm.
Cost:	N/A
Funding:	N/A
Curriculum Manager:	USJFCOM JWFC Joint Doctrine Division, Joint Training Courseware Development Branch Chief
CMDSN:	680-4388
CMCOMM:	(757) 727-4388
CMDSNFAX:	680-6552
CMCOMMFAX:	(757) 726-6552
CMCOMME-MAIL:	Artesem@jwfc.js.mil
Scheduling Activity:	N/A
SADSN:	N/A
SACOMM:	N/A
SADSNFAX:	N/A
SACOMMFAX:	N/A
SACOMME-MAIL:	N/A
Reviewing Activity:	N/A

Title:	**JFACC AUGMENTATION STAFF COURSE (JASC)**
UJTL Reference:	OP.3, OP.6
Course Number:	None
Objective:	Provides training for personnel involved with shore-based and sea-based JFACC staffs as well as potential augmentees to a JFACC organization. Focus is on staff organizations although individual attendees are accepted on a space available basis.
Description:	Utilizing multi-Service instructors, students are exposed to joint and Service doctrine, and multi-Service capabilities. Training stresses hands-on development of a 300 sortie Air Tasking Order (ATO) in a joint task force environment. Attendees use CTAPS to produce an ATO which is then translated into the Enhanced Naval Warfare Gaming System (ENWGS) enabling JFACC current operations role playing. Training format integrates academics, tabletop exercises and position-based computer wargaming.
Audience:	Personnel involved in JFACC operation, grades O3 to O6.
Clearance:	SECRET
Prerequisites:	JAOSC or prior JAOC/JFACC experience.
Length:	5 days
Frequency:	7 classes per year
Capacity:	24 students per class
Location:	Tactical Training Group, Pacific, San Diego, CA
VTC:	NONE
Distance Learning:	NONE
Cost:	Per diem and travel to the training location.
Funding:	By parent organization
Curriculum Manager:	Tactical Training Group, Pacific (POC: LtCol Monroe)
CMDSN:	553-8349
CMCOMM:	(619) 553-8349
CMDSNFAX:	553-4731
CMCOMMFAX:	(619) 553-4731
CMCOMME-MAIL:	monroelj@cod.nosc.mil
Scheduling Activity:	Tactical Training Group, Pacific (POC: CDR Koelzer)
SADSN:	553-8337
SACOMM:	(619) 553-8337
SADSNFAX:	553-4731
SACOMMFAX:	(619) 553-4731
SACOMME-MAIL:	monroelj@cod.nosc.mil
Reviewing Activity:	N/A

Title:	**TOMAHAWK LAND ATTACK MISSILE (TLAM) TACTICAL COMMANDER'S COURSE**
UJTL Reference:	OP.3; TA.3
Course Number:	CIN J-2G-007
Objective:	To train staff officers in the employment of Tomahawk, including the capabilities and limitations of the entire Tomahawk strike process, from staff planning to unit execution. The emphasis is on the planning from a Tomahawk strike coordinator's perspective.
Description:	Provides the students with an overview of the Tomahawk missile system, and details of the staff planning process, with emphasis on Tomahawk strike planning. This is accomplished through lectures and practical exercises.
Audience:	Staff officers O1-O7.
Clearance:	TOP SECRET
Prerequisites:	NONE
Length:	4 days
Frequency:	6 classes per year
Capacity:	24 students per class
Location:	TTGLANT, Dam Neck, VA
VTC:	NONE
Distance Learning:	NONE
Cost:	Per diem and travel to the training location.
Funding:	By parent organization
Curriculum Manager:	TTGLANT (POC: CDR Williams)
CMDSN:	433-7804
CMCOMM:	(757) 433-7804
CMDSNFAX:	433-6833
CMCOMMFAX:	(757) 433-6833
CMCOMME-MAIL:	
Scheduling Activity:	TTGLANT
SADSN:	433-7807
SACOMM:	(757) 433-7807
SADSNFAX:	433-6833
SACOMMFAX:	(757) 433-6833
SACOMME-MAIL:	
Reviewing Activity:	TTGLANT

Title:	**TLAM MISSION DISTRIBUTION SYSTEM COURSE (MDS)**
UJTL Reference:	OP.3, OP.5; TA.3, TA.5
Course Number:	K-2G-7000
Objective:	Develop a working knowledge of TLAM mission data dissemination and mission selection. Understand the strengths and constraints of the communication architecture. Be able to maintain and administer MDS databases and software, and be able to use MDS in the planning of a TLAM strike.
Description:	A seminar format course focusing on hands-on use of the TLAM Mission Distribution System Computer Suite. The course contains some classroom instruction and several mission selection and planning scenarios. The MDS military instruction staff is augmented by contract representatives from PRC Inc.
Audience:	OPNAV managers, JCS staff planners, Unified CINCs staff, Numbered Fleet staffs, Numbered Air Force Operations Group staff, afloat planners, task group staffs, unit commander staffs, staff cruise missile assistants (FCCS/OSCS).
Clearance:	TOP SECRET
Prerequisites:	TLAM Tactical Commander Course.
Length:	3 days
Frequency:	5 classes per year
Capacity:	10 students per class
Location:	Pt Loma Naval Complex, San Diego, CA
VTC:	NONE
Distance Learning:	NONE
Cost:	Per diem and travel to the training location.
Funding:	By parent organization
Curriculum Manager:	Tactical Training Group, Pacific (POC: CDR Tollefson)
CMDSN:	553-8341
CMCOMM:	(619) 553-8341
CMDSNFAX:	553-4731
CMCOMMFAX:	(619) 553-4731
CMCOMME-MAIL:	
Scheduling Activity:	Tactical Training Group, Pacific (POC: CDR Tollefson)
SADSN:	553-8341
SACOMM:	(619) 553-8341
SADSNFAX:	553-4731
SACOMMFAX:	(619) 553-4731
SACOMME-MAIL:	tolle@cod.nosc.mil
Reviewing Activity:	N/A

Title:	**JOINT DOCTRINE AIR CAMPAIGN COURSE**
UJTL Reference:	OP.3, OP.6; ST.3
Course Number:	MCADRE003
Objective:	A course designed for airmen from all services who have been designated, or may be designated, to serve on the staff of a Joint Force Air Component Commander (JFACC).
Description:	The course will educate airmen in the fundamental concepts, principles, and doctrine required to develop the air operations portion of a joint/combined campaign plan at the theater level.
Audience:	Airmen from all services in the grade 0-3 through 0-6 who have been designated, or may be designated, to serve on the staff of a JFACC.
Clearance:	SECRET
Prerequisites:	NONE
Length:	2 weeks
Frequency:	9 classes per year
Capacity:	45 students per class
Location:	Maxwell AFB, AL
VTC:	NONE
Distance Learning:	NONE
Cost:	Per diem and travel to the training location.
Funding:	A maximum of 324 Air Force quotas are Air University funded. All others are funded by parent organization.
Curriculum Manager:	CADRE/ARC
CMDSN:	493-4424
CMCOMM:	(334) 953-4424
CMDSNFAX:	493-4336
CMCOMMFAX:	(334) 953-4336
CMCOMME-MAIL:	
Scheduling Activity:	CADRE/ARS
SADSN:	493-5189
SACOMM:	(334) 953-5189
SADSNFAX:	493-4336
SACOMMFAX:	(334) 953-4336
SACOMME-MAIL:	
Reviewing Activity:	HQ USAF/XOCD

Title:	**MISSION DISTRIBUTION SYSTEM STAFF EMPLOYMENT COURSE (MDSSEC)**
UJTL Reference:	OP.3
Course Number:	CIN J-2F-2100
Objective:	To train staff and shipboard personnel assigned as TLAM strike officers in the use of the Mission Distribution System (MDS). The COI provides training in understanding the capabilities and limitations in using the MDS to support TLAM employment planning.
Description:	Provides the students with a working knowledge in the TLAM mission data dissemination MDS communication architecture and the ability to maintain MDS databases and software as well as the use of the MDS in TLAM strike planning. This is accomplished through lectures, laboratory work, and practical exercises.
Audience:	Officers going to a strike billet at a command that will use the MDS to assist in strike planning for grades 0-1 through 0-6.
Clearance:	TOP SECRET
Prerequisites:	Graduate of the TTCC and filling a strike billet at a command with a MDS.
Length:	3 days
Frequency:	6 classes per year
Capacity:	10 students per class
Location:	TTGLANT, Dam Neck, VA
VTC:	NONE
Distance Learning:	NONE
Cost:	Per diem and travel to the training location.
Funding:	By parent organization
Curriculum Manager:	TACTRAGRULANT (CDR Williams)
CMDSN:	433-7804
CMCOMM:	(757) 433-7804
CMDSNFAX:	433-6833
CMCOMMFAX:	(757) 433-6833
CMCOMME-MAIL:	
Scheduling Activity:	TACTRAGRULANT
SADSN:	433-7807
SACOMM:	(757) 433-7807
SADSNFAX:	433-6833
SACOMMFAX:	(757) 433-6833
SACOMME-MAIL:	
Reviewing Activity:	TACTRAGRULANT

Title:	**USCINCPAC JFACC AUGMENTEE TRAINING**
UJTL Reference:	OP.3, OP.6
Course Number:	N/A
Objective:	Provide basic doctrinal and procedural knowledge to USCINCPAC JFACC augmentees in crisis action procedures and Air Tasking Order (ATO) development.
Description:	Course is taught by a cadre of experts from all four Services using academic seminars and practical exercises to develop practice ATOs.
Audience:	Individuals designated to augment a JFACC core staff.
Clearance:	SECRET
Prerequisites:	NONE
Length:	2 days
Frequency:	Course is taught at varying locations in the Pacific four times per year (two in WESTPAC and two in EASTPAC).
Capacity:	50 students per class
Location:	Various locations
VTC:	NONE
Distance Learning:	NONE
Cost:	Per diem and travel to the training location.
Funding:	By parent organization
Curriculum Manager:	USCINCPAC J38
CMDSN:	NONE
CMCOMM:	(808) 477-3212
CMDSNFAX:	NONE
CMCOMMFAX:	(808) 477-3212
CMCOMME-MAIL:	
Scheduling Activity:	USCINCPAC J38
SADSN:	NONE
SACOMM:	(808) 477-3212
SADSNFAX:	NONE
SACOMMFAX:	(808) 477-2851
SACOMME-MAIL:	
Reviewing Activity:	N/A

Title:	**JOINT COURSE ON LOGISTICS**
UJTL Reference:	OP.4
Course Number:	ALMC-JC
Objective:	To prepare military officers and civilians to function in assignments which involve joint logistics planning, inter-Service and multinational logistics support, and joint logistics in a theater of operations.
Description:	Integrates component functional skills and knowledge through the study of strategy, doctrine, theory, programs and processes, and provides the opportunity for students to develop the attitudes, perspectives, and insights necessary to manage logistics at the operational level of war.
Audience:	04-05; GS12-14.
Clearance:	NONE
Prerequisites:	Mid-level managers assigned to or enroute to a joint logistics assignment.
Length:	2 weeks, 3 days
Frequency:	15 classes per year
Capacity:	40 students per class
Location:	ALMC, Ft. Lee, VA
VTC:	NONE
Distance Learning:	NONE
Cost:	Per diem and travel to the training location.
Funding:	By parent organization
Curriculum Manager:	ALMC (POC: Mr. Chadwick)
CMDSN:	539-4710
CMCOMM:	NONE
CMDSNFAX:	539-4663/4647
CMCOMMFAX:	N/A
CMCOMME-MAIL:	
Scheduling Activity:	ALMC (POC: Mr. Chadwick)
SADSN:	539-4710
SACOMM:	NONE
SADSNFAX:	539-4663/4647
SACOMMFAX:	N/A
SACOMME-MAIL:	
Reviewing Activity:	N/A

Title:	**JOINT EMPLOYMENT MULTIMEDIA CD-ROM**
UJTL Reference:	OP.4
Course Number:	N/A
Objective:	The primary purpose of this effort is to enhance the overall awareness of joint doctrine using state-of-the-art technology.
Description:	This interactive multimedia product focuses on the concepts and principles of operational art as well as aspects of joint force employment including considerations before and during combat, joint air operations, logistics, intelligence, information operations, military operations other than war, planning, and special operations. Drawing reference materials directly from approved joint doctrine; the multimedia CSD-ROM will ensure doctrine accuracy and consistency without interpretation and will be designed to improve knowledge about joint doctrine.
Audience:	Military service members, civilians.
Clearance:	N/A
Prerequisites:	N/A
Length:	N/A
Frequency:	N/A
Capacity:	N/A
Location:	N/A
VTC:	N/A
Distance Learning:	N/A
Cost:	N/A
Funding:	N/A
Curriculum Manager:	N/A
CMDSN:	N/A
CMCOMM:	N/A
CMDSNFAX:	N/A
CMCOMMFAX:	N/A
CMCOMME-MAIL:	N/A
Scheduling Activity:	N/A
SADSN:	N/A
SACOMM:	N/A
SADSNFAX:	N/A
SACOMMFAX:	N/A
SACOMME-MAIL:	N/A
Reviewing Activity:	N/A

Title:	**JOINT DOCTRINE AWARENESS ACTION PLAN**
UJTL Reference:	OP.4
Course Number:	N/A
Objective:	To make the joint community more aware of joint doctrine.
Description:	The CJCS tasked Joint Staff, JDD, to develop an action plan that would enhance the overall awareness of joint doctrine throughout the armed forces and keep joint doctrine at the forefront of professional dialogue. The plan outline includes a series of professionally developed products to accomplish the CJCS tasking. The plan uses a building block approach in which each new product builds and expands upon previous products. This accommodates new doctrine as well as changes to existing doctrine. Consequently, not only is currency of new products ensured, but also development efficiencies and product quality are improved.
Audience:	Military service members, civilians.
Clearance:	N/A
Prerequisites:	N/A
Length:	N/A
Frequency:	N/A
Capacity:	N/A
Location:	N/A
VTC:	N/A
Distance Learning:	N/A
Cost:	N/A
Funding:	N/A
Curriculum Manager:	LtCol Steven Taylor, Joint Staff/J-7, Joint Doctrine Division
CMDSN:	224-6493
CMCOMM:	N/A
CMDSNFAX:	N/A
CMCOMMFAX:	N/A
CMCOMME-MAIL:	N/A
Scheduling Activity:	N/A
SADSN:	N/A
SACOMM:	N/A
SADSNFAX:	N/A
SACOMMFAX:	N/A
SACOMME-MAIL:	N/A
Reviewing Activity:	N/A

Title:	**JOINT FORCE EMPLOYMENT MODULES**
UJTL Reference:	OP.4
Course Number:	N/A
Objective:	To familiarize individuals with various aspects of joint force employment and joint operations.
Description:	The briefing modules consist of a complete script and corresponding graphics. Specific modules have been created on joint force employment, operational art, planning, joint air operations, special operations, logistic support operations, information operations, considerations before and during combat, intelligence support operations, and military operations other than war. These briefing modules provide an excellent source for either group presentation or individual study.
Audience:	Military service members, civilians.
Clearance:	N/A
Prerequisites:	N/A
Length:	N/A
Frequency:	N/A
Capacity:	N/A
Location:	N/A
VTC:	N/A
Distance Learning:	Available on the JEL and JEL CD-ROM.
Cost:	N/A
Funding:	N/A
Curriculum Manager:	N/A
CMDSN:	N/A
CMCOMM:	N/A
CMDSNFAX:	N/A
CMCOMMFAX:	N/A
CMCOMME-MAIL:	N/A
Scheduling Activity:	N/A
SADSN:	N/A
SACOMM:	N/A
SADSNFAX:	N/A
SACOMMFAX:	N/A
SACOMME-MAIL:	N/A
Reviewing Activity:	N/A

Title:	**JOINT DOCTRINE ENCYCLOPEDIA**
UJTL Reference:	OP.4
Course Number:	N/A
Objective:	This volume provides a convenient reference source for joint doctrine concepts and is intended to benefit users at all levels, including professional military education students, action officers, and planners.
Description:	The encyclopedia consists of approximately 1000 terms, each cross-referenced to other related terms as well as the source publications. In addition, vignettes, graphics, and photos enhance readability. The encyclopedia is available on the JEL and CD-ROM.
Audience:	Military service members, civilians.
Clearance:	N/A
Prerequisites:	N/A
Length:	N/A
Frequency:	N/A
Capacity:	N/A
Location:	N/A
VTC:	N/A
Distance Learning:	N/A
Cost:	N/A
Funding:	N/A
Curriculum Manager:	N/A
CMDSN:	N/A
CMCOMM:	N/A
CMDSNFAX:	N/A
CMCOMMFAX:	N/A
CMCOMME-MAIL:	N/A
Scheduling Activity:	N/A
SADSN:	N/A
SACOMM:	N/A
SADSNFAX:	N/A
SACOMMFAX:	N/A
SACOMME-MAIL:	N/A
Reviewing Activity:	N/A

Title:	**JOINT MILITARY OPERATIONS HISTORICAL COLLECTION**
UJTL Reference:	OP.4
Course Number:	N/A
Objective:	To provide a compendium of military actions, doctrine and principles for ready reference.
Description:	This publication is a selection of seven case histories of military actions, each illustrative of the fundamentals of joint doctrine principles. The collection complements joint doctrine, highlighting the lessons that these historical operations have taught and encouraging original thought and effective response to future military challenges. The collection is available on the JEL and JEL CD-ROM.
Audience:	Military service members, civilians.
Clearance:	N/A
Prerequisites:	N/A
Length:	N/A
Frequency:	N/A
Capacity:	N/A
Location:	N/A
VTC:	N/A
Distance Learning:	N/A
Cost:	N/A
Funding:	N/A
Curriculum Manager:	N/A
CMDSN:	N/A
CMCOMM:	N/A
CMDSNFAX:	N/A
CMCOMMFAX:	N/A
CMCOMME-MAIL:	N/A
Scheduling Activity:	N/A
SADSN:	N/A
SACOMM:	N/A
SADSNFAX:	N/A
SACOMMFAX:	N/A
SACOMME-MAIL:	N/A
Reviewing Activity:	N/A

Title:	**JOINT MARITIME TACTICS COURSE**
UJTL Reference:	OP.5
Course Number:	CIN J-2G-3009
Objective:	Provide appropriate experienced flag and senior naval officers the current tactical knowledge and practical skills required to plan and execute naval task force and navy battle group combat operations within a joint task force. With the goal of battlespace dominance and mission success, the focus is on: force employment decision making and interaction between the officer in tactical command (OTC), composite warfare commander (CWC), and warfare commanders/coordinators within the naval architecture; the coordination and interaction between the naval component/maritime component commander and the joint force commander and other Service/functional component commanders within the joint force architecture.
Description:	Course addresses various aspects of maritime warfare with a primary focus on Carrier Battle Group (CVBG) and Amphibious Ready Group (ARG) operations in a littoral environment. Emphasis is to assist the warfare commander and staff with planning, decision making and address Naval Force (NAVFOR) integration into a Joint Task Force (JTF). Course consists of two weeks of planning as the NAVOFR in a likely Pacific Command JTF scenario, culminating in two days of war gaming. War gaming employs both "table top" and Enhanced Naval Warfare Gaming System (ENWGS) methods to execute class' overall strategy, warfare specific pre-planned responses, stress command and control issues, asset employment and tactics at the warfare command level.
Audience:	Prospective battlegroup commanders, amphibious/destroyer/aircraft squadron commanders, ship/submarine commanding officers, and all their principal staff officers. Students consist of all naval warfare specialties and afloat warfare support specialties in grades 0-4 through 0-7.
Clearance:	TOP SECRET/SCI and SECRET
Prerequisites:	Embedded officer community screening and orders to targeted billets.
Length:	3 weeks
Frequency:	8 classes per year
Capacity:	328 students per class
Location:	Building #58, Fleet Training Center, Point Loma, San Diego, CA
VTC:	NONE
Distance Learning:	NONE
Cost:	Per diem and travel to the training location.
Funding:	By parent organization

Curriculum Manager:	Tactical Training Group (POC: CDR Jack Miller)
CMDSN:	553-9948
CMCOMM:	(619) 553-9948
CMDSNFAX:	
CMCOMMFAX:	
CMCOMME-MAIL:	SIPRNET USWSYN@FCTCPAC.NAVY.SMIL.MIL
Scheduling Activity:	Tactical Training Group, Pacific (POC: Mr. Jamie Cotto)
SADSN:	553-8337
SACOMM:	(619) 553-8337
SADSNFAX:	
SACOMMFAX:	
SACOMME-MAIL:	
Reviewing Activity:	N/A

Title:	**JOINT MARITIME TACTICS COURSE**
UJTL Reference:	OP.3, OP.5, OP.6; TA.1, TA.3, TA.5
Course Number:	K-2G-3009
Objective:	Provide appropriate experienced flag and senior officers with the current tactical knowledge and practical skills required to plan and execute Battle Group/Force Combat Operations, including joint operations. Stress the interaction between the CJTF and the OTC, Composite Warfare Commander, and their subordinate warfare commanders, as well as joint task force components and the other Services.
Description:	Course consists of two weeks of formal classroom instruction and one week of wargaming. Addresses all aspects of maritime warfare with a primary focus on Carrier Battle Group Operations in a littoral environment and as the naval component of joint task force operations. Course structure includes a series of classroom presentations by in-house subject discussions. The course culminates in wargaming a joint scenario highlighting a likely PACOM mission utilizing the Enhanced Naval Warfare Gaming System (ENWGS).
Audience:	Attendance required for naval officers enroute to command and key staff billets in the Pacific. Recommended for all officers who interact with the US Navy or who require a greater understanding of the US Navy and what the Navy Component Commander brings to joint task force operations (Grades O-4 to O-8).
Clearance:	SECRET
Prerequisites:	NONE
Length:	3 weeks
Frequency:	10 classes per year
Capacity:	40 students per class
Location:	Pt Loma Naval Complex, San Diego, CA
VTC:	NONE
Distance Learning:	NONE
Cost:	Per diem and travel to the training location.
Funding:	By parent organization
Curriculum Manager:	Tactical Training Group, Pacific (POC: LCDR Manduley)
CMDSN:	553-8341
CMCOMM:	(619) 553-8341
CMDSNFAX:	553-4731
CMCOMMFAX:	(619) 553-4731
CMCOMME-MAIL:	ttgplib@nosc.mil
Scheduling Activity:	Tactical Training Group, Pacific (POC: LCDR Manduley)
SADSN:	553-8341
SACOMM:	(619) 553-8341
SADSNFAX:	553-4731
SACOMMFAX:	(619) 553-4731
SACOMME-MAIL:	ttgplib@nosc.mil
Reviewing Activity:	N/A

Title:	**ACADEMIC TRAINING SEMINARS (UNIFIED ENDEAVOR EXERCISES)**
UJTL Reference:	OP.5; ST.5
Course Number:	N/A
Objective:	To provide the necessary academic training and educational opportunities for core and augmentee elements of Joint Task Force (JTF) commanders/staffs and functional component commanders/staffs to prepare them for participation in all phases of the USJFCOM Tier 3 Joint Command Training Program via the UNIFIED ENDEAVOR (UE) exercises.
Description:	The academic seminars are conducted at the USJFCOM Joint Training, Analysis and Simulation Center (JTASC), Suffolk, VA, during the three phases of USJFCOM UE exercises. Phase I (four days) consists entirely of seminars which provide the JTF commanders and functional component commanders and their principal staffs with academic and team-building opportunities in a variety of areas associated with the conduct of joint operations, e.g., Forming a JTF Headquarters, JTF Organization and Command Relationships, Joint Operational Planning Process. They are built around vignettes which provide the staff an opportunity to discuss solutions to key exercise-related issues. Phase II (academic portion - one day) provides functional-level seminars for the JTF principal staff planners prior to their developing an Operations Order. Phase III (Academic portion - one-half day) provides the staff with training which prepares them to execute the operation order in a computer simulation driven exercise. Seminar content may be customized to support either US joint training or joint/multinational training. The emphasis in all seminars is on joint lessons learned and emerging issues in joint operations. Seminars in Phases II and III are less formally structured than those in Phase I.
Audience:	UE participants, to include USJFCOM standing or potential JTF commanders/staffs and functional component commanders/ staffs; other forces assigned to USJFCOM for JTF training; and JTF commanders/staffs assigned to other CINCs, if requested. Seminar participants come from all Services and include 0-5 to 0-9 (Phase I), 0-4 to 0-6 (Phase II), and E-5 to 0-6 (Phase III).
Clearance:	Up to SECRET; most seminars are unclassified.
Prerequisites:	Must be a designated member of a UE conducted/ supporting by USJFCOM.
Length:	Phase I seminars: 1-2 hours each; Phase II and III seminars: 1/2 to 2 hours each.
Frequency:	Up to four major UEs (Phases I-III) and four minor UEs (Phases I/II only) per year.
Capacity:	Varies according to phase; Phase I-90; Phase II-250; Phase III-500.
Location:	Suffolk, VA

VTC:

Distance Learning:	Capability to broadcast from the JTASC to various remote sites.
Cost:	CONUS/OCONUS training audience sites.
Funding:	Through VTC during Phase I seminars, as applicable.
	Per diem and travel as required. Funded through UE
Curriculum Manager:	Exercise series and Service OMA funds.
CMDSN:	USJFCOM, J-75 (J75ISD)
CMCOMM:	564-9100, ext 7296
CMDSNFAX:	(757) 686-7296
CMCOMMFAX:	564-9100, ext. 7253
CMCOMME-MAIL:	(757) 686-7253
Scheduling Activity:	kuehl@acom.mil
SADSN:	USJFCOM, J-72 (J722)
SACOMM:	564-9100, ext 7217
SADSNFAX:	(757) 686-7217
SACOMMFAX:	564-9100, ext 7253
SACOMME-MAIL:	(757) 686-7253
Reviewing Activity:	engle@acom.mil
	N/A

Title:	**JOINT COMMAND, CONTROL, COMMUNICATIONS, COMPUTERS, AND INTELLIGENCE STAFF AND OPERATIONS COURSE (JC4ISOC)**
UJTL Reference:	OP.5; ST.5; SN.5
Course Number:	S-00-3334
Objective:	To acquaint middle grade officers and equivalent DOD civilians with C4I concepts in the joint environment, the DOD's organization and how it supports the C4I process, and the management and operation of current joint C4I systems and attendant joint operational procedures associated with both strategic and theater/tactical systems.
Description:	The JC4ISOC curriculum is designed for the non-technically oriented student, covering a broad range of national, strategic, theater, and tactical C4I topics, from the National Military Command System to the joint task force planning and direct warfighter support. The primary method of instruction is lecture with guided discussion. Field trips to local area and Washington, D.C. locations reinforce classroom material and provide the students a "hands-on" opportunity. Guest lecturers are used extensively to bring an indepth knowledge of specific subjects and current information to the class.
Audience:	W-1 through O-6 officers and civilian equivalent assigned to key command, control, and communications positions throughout DOD.
Clearance:	TOP SECRET/SCI
Prerequisites:	NONE
Length:	5 weeks
Frequency:	6 classes per year
Capacity:	25 students per class
Location:	AFSC, Norfolk, VA
VTC:	In development
Distance Learning:	NONE
Cost:	Per diem and travel to the training location.
Funding:	By parent organization
Curriculum Manager:	AFSC (POC: LTC Long)
CMDSN:	564-5142
CMCOMM:	(757) 444-5142
CMDSNFAX:	564-6381
CMCOMMFAX:	(757) 444-6381
CMCOMME-MAIL:	
Scheduling Activity:	AFSC (POC: LTC Long)
SADSN:	564-5142
SACOMM:	(757) 444-5142
SADSNFAX:	564-6381
SACOMMFAX:	N/A
SACOMME-MAIL:	long@afscmail.afsc.edu
Reviewing Activity:	Joint Staff Review

Title:	**ACC JFCC--JOINT FIREPOWER CONTROL COURSE (JFCC)**
UJTL Reference:	OP.5; TA.5
Course Number:	N/A
Objective:	To train jointly approved concepts, doctrine, procedures, and techniques for integrating combat efforts to services in joint operations.
Description:	JFCC is an interservice training course designed to teach jointly approved procedures and techniques used to plan, request, coordinate, and control joint firepower. It provides a general overview of the Theater Air Control System (TACS) and Army Air Ground System (AAGS). The course focuses on firepower and force integration functions performed by Army, Navy, Marine, Air Force, and Special Forces personnel at US ground force echelons at division level and below. Emphasis is on training selected officers and enlisted personnel, primarily Army and Air Force, to effectively function in the Theater Air Control System (TACS)/Army Air Ground System (AAGS).
Audience:	Theater Air Control personnel: All air liaison officers (ALOs) assigned to division level and below and all forward air controllers (FACs). Air Mobility Command (AMC) personnel: Theater airlift liaison officers (TALOs) assigned to work at Army command echelons. Army personnel: Mandatory for personnel assigned to duties requiring 5U ASI. Marines assigned as Air Liaison Officers, Forward Air Controllers, Fire Support Coordination Center (FSCC), Artillery, and Naval Gunfire personnel. Navy personnel: Air Operations, Intelligence, Electronic Warfare, and Communication Officers assigned to Commander Amphibious Group (AMPHIBGRU One/Two/Three and Tactical Control Squadron) Command Element and Supporting Arms Coordination Center (SACC).
Clearance:	SECRET
Prerequisites:	Air Force personnel assigned or selected for assignment for duty as an ALO, FAC, TALO, or Enlisted Terminal Attack Controller (ETAC). Army personnel assigned to, or selected for, duty involving the air ground operations system at Corps level and below. Navy personnel assigned to the Navy amphibious forces whose duties and responsibilities are related to command, control, communications, or intelligence in fixed wing (airborne forward air controller)/ helicopter, naval gunfire, or artillery fire support. Marine Corps personnel assigned to Fleet Marine Forces whose duties and responsibilities are related to command, control, communication, or intelligence in fixed wing/ helicopter, naval gunfire, or artillery fire support.
Length:	15 days
Frequency:	7 classes per year
Capacity:	100 students per class
Location:	Nellis AFB, NV

VTC:	NONE
Distance Learning:	NONE
Cost:	Per diem and travel to the training location.
Funding:	By parent Service or organization
Curriculum Manager:	USAFAGOS JFCC/CC (Lt. Col Matte)
CMDSN:	682-8560
CMCOMM:	(702) 652-8560
CMDSNFAX:	682-4298
CMCOMMFAX:	(702) 652-4298
CMCOMME-MAIL:	jfcc/cc@nellis.af.mil
Scheduling Activity:	USAFAGOS JFCC/CCQ (TSgt Wilson)
SADSN:	682-9474
SACOMM:	(702) 652-4298
SADSNFAX:	682-4298
SACOMMFAX:	(702) 652-4298
SACOMME-MAIL:	jfcc/ccq@nellis.af.mil
Reviewing Activity:	USAFAGOS

Title:	**CTAPS BASIC OPERATOR'S COURSE (CBOC)**
UJTL Reference:	OP.3, OP.5; TA.3, TA.5
Course Number:	NONE
Objective:	Train personnel in basic operation of CTAPS, the ATO generation tool.
Description:	Provides hands-on training for Contingency Theater Automated Planning System (CTAPS) operators. Introduces attendees to most common CTAPS modules (HMI, CAFMS, APS, ADS, RAAP). Course format provides academic instruction followed by lengthy hands-on training using a JAOC configured CTAPS suite. Focus is on developing operator skills to quickly and efficiently enter raw ATO data and produce a completed ATO.
Audience:	ATO production cell members, grades E-4 to O-3.
Clearance:	SECRET
Prerequisites:	NONE
Length:	3 days
Frequency:	7 classes per year
Capacity:	24 students per class (limited by CTAPS availability of 2 students per machine).
Location:	Tactical Training Group Pacific, San Diego, CA
VTC:	NONE
Distance Learning:	NONE
Cost:	Per diem and travel to the training location.
Funding:	By parent organization
Curriculum Manager:	Tactical Training Group, Pacific (POC: Lt Mike Flood)
CMDSN:	553-8807
CMCOMM:	(619) 553-8807
CMDSNFAX:	553-4731
CMCOMMFAX:	(619) 553-4731
CMCOMME-MAIL:	floodm@nosc.mil
Scheduling Activity:	Tactical Training Group, Pacific (POC: Mr. Jamie Cotto)
SADSN:	553-8337
SACOMM:	(619) 553-8337
SADSNFAX:	553-4731
SACOMMFAX:	(619) 553-4731
SACOMME-MAIL:	ttgplib@nosc.mil
Reviewing Activity:	N/A

Title:	**JOINT TACTICAL INFORMATION DISTRIBUTION SYSTEM (JTIDS)**
UJTL Reference:	OP.5; TA.5
Course Number:	JT-101
Objective:	To train personnel in the planning, employment, and operating procedures of the Joint Tactical Information Distribution System (JTIDS).
Description:	Provide training in joint planning, employment, operating procedures and systems capabilities of the Joint Tactical Information System (JTIDS).
Audience:	E-4 through O-4 and civilian personnel operators, planners, and designers.
Clearance:	SECRET
Prerequisites:	NONE
Length:	3 days/24 hours
Frequency:	2 times a quarter
Capacity:	15-20 students per class
Location:	Ft. McPherson, GA
VTC:	NONE
Distance Learning:	NONE
Cost:	Per diem and travel to the training location.
Funding:	USN--CNET N8455 (DSN 922-3684); USAF--HQ ACC/DOY (DSN 574-8328); USMC--HQMC (Code APC)(DSN 224-1850); USA--FORSCOM AFOP-JTS (DSN 572-4646).
Curriculum Manager:	AFOP-JT (POC: CW3 Jaycox)
CMDSN:	367-4626
CMCOMM:	(404) 464-4626
CMDSNFAX:	367-4632/4608
CMCOMMFAX:	(404) 464-4632/4608
CMCOMME-MAIL:	
Scheduling Activity:	AFOP-JT
SADSN:	367-4626
SACOMM:	(404) 464-4626
SADSNFAX:	367-4632/4608
SACOMMFAX:	(404) 464-4632/4608
SACOMME-MAIL:	
Reviewing Activity:	N/A

Title:	**MULTI-TADIL ADVANCED JOINT INTEROPERABILITY COURSE (MAJIC)**
UJTL Reference:	OP.5; TA.5
Course Number:	JT-102
Objective:	To train jointly approved concepts, doctrine, procedures, and techniques for integrating, operating, and managing Multiple Tactical Digital Information Links in joint operations.
Description:	Provides detailed information on Tactical Digital Information Links (TADILs) operation and management, and Tactical Data Systems (TDS) utilized in the Services. Includes message formats, systems capabilities and limitations, operational and planning requirements of the TADILs utilized in a joint operation.
Audience:	Service TADIL operators and planners (E-4 through O-4).
Clearance:	SECRET
Prerequisites:	NONE
Length:	15 days
Frequency:	Monthly (except April and December)
Capacity:	15 students per class
Location:	Ft. McPherson, GA
VTC:	NONE
Distance Learning:	NONE
Cost:	Per diem and travel to the training location.
Funding:	USN--CNET N8455 (DSN: 922-3684); USAF--HQ ACC/DOY (DSN: 574-8328); USMC--JQMC (Code APC)(DSN 224-1850; USA--FORSCOM AFOP (DSN 572-4646).
Curriculum Manager:	AFOP-JT (CW3 Jaycox)
CMDSN:	367-4626
CMCOMM:	(404) 464-4626
CMDSNFAX:	367-4632/4608
CMCOMMFAX:	(404) 464-4632/4608
CMCOMME-MAIL:	
Scheduling Activity:	AFOP-JT
SADSN:	367-4626
SACOMM:	(404) 464-4626
SADSNFAX:	367-4632/4608
SACOMMFAX:	(404) 464-4632/4608
SACOMME-MAIL:	
Reviewing Activity:	N/A

Title:	**JOINT TACTICAL INFORMATION DISTRIBUTION SYSTEM (JTIDS) NETWORK DESIGN AND SYSTEM MANAGEMENT**
UJTL Reference:	OP.5; TA.5
Course Number:	JT-201
Objective:	Introduce students to joint JTIDS network planning, design, and evaluation.
Description:	Train unit level JTIDS network planners, joint multi-TADIL network planners, and unit level deconfliction managers in JTIDS network management, planning, design and deconfliction procedures. To train students in joint JTIDS network design concepts, applications, and network design aids.
Audience:	Operational planners, JTIDS network designers.
Clearance:	SECRET
Prerequisites:	JT-101 or JT-102.
Length:	5 days
Frequency:	Quarterly
Capacity:	10 students per class
Location:	Ft. McPherson, GA
VTC:	NONE
Distance Learning:	NONE
Cost:	Per diem and travel to the training location.
Funding:	USN--CNET N8455 (DSN: 922-3684); USAF--HQ ACC/DOY (DSN: 574-8328); USMC--JQMC (Code APC)(DSN 224-1850; USA--FORSCOM AFOP (DSN 572-4646).
Curriculum Manager:	AFOP-JT (CW3 Jaycox)
CMDSN:	367-4626
CMCOMM:	(404) 464-4626
CMDSNFAX:	367-4632/4608
CMCOMMFAX:	(404) 464-4632/4608
CMCOMME-MAIL:	
Scheduling Activity:	AFOP-JT
SADSN:	367-4626
SACOMM:	(404) 464-4626
SADSNFAX:	367-4632/4608
SACOMMFAX:	(404) 464-4632/4608
SACOMME-MAIL:	
Reviewing Activity:	N/A

Title:	**JOINT TASK FORCE HEADQUARTERS MASTER TRAINING GUIDE (JTF HQ MTG) (CJCSM 3500.05)**
UJTL Reference:	OP.1, OP.2, OP.3, OP.4, OP.5, OP.6
Course Number:	N/A
Objective:	To provide probable or designated JTF commanders and staffs with guidance and assistance in planning for, conducting, and assessing JTF HQ training and operations.
Description:	The JTF HQ MTG is a joint courseware product which consists of a series of tasks describing in detail what is required to operate as a JTF HQ. It is based upon the Universal Joint Task List (UJTL) and organized according to the life cycle of a JTF: forming, planning, deploying, employing, transitioning, and redeploying. It links the tasks in the UJTL with the procedures in joint doctrine/JTTP for a specific training audience -- a JTF HQ. It contains matrices which pinpoint who and what needs to be trained, helping users locate and cross-reference task information. The "core" of the JTF HQ MTG (Chapter 5) consists of outlines for each task performed by the JTF HQ command and staff elements. It also contains a description of the task, applicable references, and detailed task steps. CJCSM 3500.05 reflects Version 2.6 of the JTF HQ MTG. Draft Version 3.0 (Chapter 5, Section II – Plans and Orders)(Aug 97) is currently being piloted and is available by contacting the Curriculum Manager listed below.
Audience:	JTF commanders and staffs.
Clearance:	Unclassified
Prerequisites:	N/A
Length:	N/A
Frequency:	N/A
Capacity:	N/A
Location:	N/A
VTC:	N/A
Distance Learning:	http://www.dtic.mil/doctrine/jel/cjcsd/cjcsm.htm
Cost:	N/A
Funding:	N/A
Curriculum Manager:	USJFCOM J75 (Ms. Linda Kuehl, J75 ISD)
CMDSN:	564-9100, ext 7296
CMCOMM:	(757) 686-7296
CMDSNFAX:	564-9100, ext 7253
CMCOMMFAX:	(757) 686-7253
CMCOMME-MAIL:	kuehl@acom.mil
Scheduling Activity:	N/A
SADSN:	N/A
SACOMM:	N/A
SADSNFAX:	N/A
SACOMMFAX:	N/A
SACOMME-MAIL:	N/A
Reviewing Activity:	N/A

Title:	**ANTITERRORISM INSTRUCTOR QUALIFICATION**
UJTL Reference:	OP.6; TA.6
Course Number:	5K-F5/012-F30
Objective:	N/A
Description:	Terrorism and terrorist operations; individual protective measures; hostage survival techniques and terrorist surveillance detection.
Audience:	Must be a member of the Active or Reserve component of the US Armed Forces or a DOD civilian (NOFORN).
Clearance:	NONE
Prerequisites:	Must be an experienced instructor; USA and USMC personnel must be the rank of SSG or above; USAF personnel must be in the rank of TSGT or above; USN personnel must be in the rank of PO-1 or above; DOD civilians must be in the grade of GS-7 or above. Individuals should have at least two years' retention in their present assignment. USA personnel must complete TABE Level A within three months prior to attending the course.
Length:	1 week - 4 days
Frequency:	6 times per year
Capacity:	72 per year
Location:	JFK Special Warfare Center and School, Ft. Bragg, NC
VTC:	NONE
Distance Learning:	NONE
Cost:	Transportation plus per diem.
Funding:	Parent unit
Curriculum Manager:	Commander, A Company, 2nd Battalion, 1st SWTG (A)
CMDSN:	239-5456
CMCOMM:	N/A
CMDSNFAX:	239-5618
CMCOMMFAX:	N/A
CMCOMME-MAIL:	
Scheduling Activity:	USASOC, DCSOPS
SADSN:	239-3676
SACOMM:	N/A
SADSNFAX:	239-5866
SACOMMFAX:	N/A
SACOMME-MAIL:	
Reviewing Activity:	N/A

Title:	**INDIVIDUAL TERRORISM AWARENESS**
UJTL Reference:	OP.6; TA.6
Course Number:	3A-F40/011-F21
Objective:	N/A
Description:	Terrorism and terrorist operations; self-protection measures; hostage survival techniques.
Audience:	Active duty military personnel, federal government employees, and adult family member (NOFORN).
Clearance:	SECRET
Prerequisites:	Must be presently assigned to or enroute to an overseas area outside US military installations where a moderate-to-high terrorist threat exists. Sponsors must initiate the process for each of their adult family members to obtain a security clearance.
Length:	1 week
Frequency:	24 per year
Capacity:	500 per year
Location:	Ft. Bragg, NC
VTC:	NONE
Distance Learning:	NONE
Cost:	Transportation plus per diem.
Funding:	Parent unit
Curriculum Manager:	Commander, A Company, 2nd Battalion, 1st SWTG (A)
CMDSN:	239-5456
CMCOMM:	N/A
CMDSNFAX:	239-5618
CMCOMMFAX:	N/A
CMCOMME-MAIL:	
Scheduling Activity:	USASOC, DCSOPS
SADSN:	239-3676
SACOMM:	N/A
SADSNFAX:	239-5866
SACOMMFAX:	N/A
SACOMME-MAIL:	
Reviewing Activity:	N/A

Title:	**ENLISTED INTELLIGENCE MID-CAREER COURSE (EIMCC)**
UJTL Reference:	TA.2
Course Number:	J-150-2967
Objective:	Expose mid-level and senior enlisted intelligence personnel to intelligence issues and technologies at the tactical and organizational level.
Description:	Focuses on the role of the intelligence specialist, new technologies/equipment, manpower issues, joint warfare/operations, fleet perspectives/issues, and intelligence community developments. Topics presented by senior intelligence personnel.
Audience:	Enlisted intelligence personnel E-6 and above.
Clearance:	SECRET
Prerequisites:	A 3-5 page unclassified paper on an intelligence related topic is required to be submitted upon class convening.
Length:	5 days
Frequency:	4 classes per year
Capacity:	25 students per class
Location:	NMITC, Dam Neck, VA
VTC:	NONE
Distance Learning:	NONE
Cost:	Per diem and travel to the training location.
Funding:	By parent organization
Curriculum Manager:	NMITC (Lt Rigazzi)
CMDSN:	433-0019
CMCOMM:	(757) 433-0019
CMDSNFAX:	433-0336
CMCOMMFAX:	(757) 433-0336
CMCOMME-MAIL:	
Scheduling Activity:	NMITC
SADSN:	433-0126
SACOMM:	(757) 433-0126
SADSNFAX:	N/A
SACOMMFAX:	N/A
SACOMME-MAIL:	
Reviewing Activity:	CNET

Title:	**ELECTRONIC WARFARE APPLICATIONS (ADVANCED)**
UJTL Reference:	TA.5
Course Number:	A-230-0018
Objective:	To teach reasons and interrelationships that exist within the structure of the EW integration operational scenario.
Description:	Provides senior EW personnel with the knowledge and skills necessary to integrate and tactically employ shipboard total force EW sensor assets in support of command and control warfare (C2W), and command and control warfare commander (C2WC) concept; coordinate the integration of EW equipment with other shipboard combat and weapons systems; integrate and plan battle force/battle group EW in support of allied and joint operations; coordinate with warfare commanders/communities for assets; plan and execute battle force training; and prepare EW related correspondence and support of multi-ship operations to include equipment acquisition and various planning documents.
Audience:	EW technician E-7 to E-9.
Clearance:	SECRET
Prerequisites:	Must be EW Technician.
Length:	40 days
Frequency:	5 classes per year
Capacity:	8 students per class
Location:	Pensacola, FL
VTC:	NONE
Distance Learning:	NONE
Cost:	Per diem and travel to the training location.
Funding:	By parent organization
Curriculum Manager:	CNEWS
CMDSN:	922-6528
CMCOMM:	(850) 452-4921
CMDSNFAX:	922-6843
CMCOMMFAX:	(850) 452-6843
CMCOMME-MAIL:	
Scheduling Activity:	PERS - 406C
SADSN:	227-1147
SACOMM:	(703) 697-1147
SADSNFAX:	223-3544
SACOMMFAX:	N/A
SACOMME-MAIL:	
Reviewing Activity:	CNET

Title:	**JOINT TACTICAL INFORMATION DISTRIBUTION SYSTEMS (JTIDS) INTRODUCTION**
UJTL Reference:	TA.5
Course Number:	K-2G-0167
Objective:	Familiarize the student with an in-depth overview of the purposes, capabilities and functions of Link-16.
Description:	Informational instruction. Format is lectures/discussion/ visual references.
Audience:	E-5 through 0-5 data systems managers, operators and specialists on new installation units, embarked staffs and prior K-2G-0168.
Clearance:	SECRET
Prerequisites:	NONE
Length:	2 days
Frequency:	4 classes per year
Capacity:	25 students per class
Location:	FCTCPAC, San Diego, CA
VTC:	NONE
Distance Learning:	NONE
Cost:	Per diem and travel to the training location.
Funding:	By parent organization
Curriculum Manager:	FCTC Pacific
CMDSN:	553-8302
CMCOMM:	(619) 553-8302
CMDSNFAX:	553-8127
CMCOMMFAX:	(619) 553-8127
CMCOMME-MAIL:	
Scheduling Activity:	FCTC Pacific
SADSN:	553-8302
SACOMM:	(619) 553-8302
SADSNFAX:	553-8127
SACOMMFAX:	(619) 553-8127
SACOMME-MAIL:	
Reviewing Activity:	N/A

Title:	**NAVY TACTICAL COMMAND SYSTEMS AFLOAT (NTCS-A) MANAGER**
UJTL Reference:	TA.5
Course Number:	J-2G-2302
Objective:	To train personnel how to manage Navy Tactical Command Systems – Afloat (NTCS-A) equipment and data using NTCS-A hardware and software installed in the fleet.
Description:	Consists of classroom presentations and practical work encompassing: Over-the-horizon targeting (OTHT) concepts; communication net-works; shore and afloat nodes; tactical data processor (TDP) interoperability; operation of TDPs and associated software; database management; tactical decision aid (TDA) functions; information exchange systems (OTCIXS/TADIXS); battle group organization and operations.
Audience:	E-6 through 0-5.
Clearance:	SECRET
Prerequisites:	NONE
Length:	5 days
Frequency:	36 classes per year
Capacity:	30 students per class
Location:	FCTCLANT Dam Neck, VA
VTC:	NONE
Distance Learning:	NONE
Cost:	Per diem and travel to the training location.
Funding:	By parent organization
Curriculum Manager:	FCTCLANT Dam Neck
CMDSN:	433-7446
CMCOMM:	(757) 433-7446
CMDSNFAX:	433-6613
CMCOMMFAX:	(757) 433-6613
CMCOMME-MAIL:	
Scheduling Activity:	FCTCLANT Dam Neck
SADSN:	433-6613
SACOMM:	(757) 433-7758
SADSNFAX:	433-7759
SACOMMFAX:	(757) 433-7759
SACOMME-MAIL:	
Reviewing Activity:	N/A

Title:	**NAVY TACTICAL COMMAND SYSTEMS AFLOAT (NTCS-A) OPERATOR**
UJTL Reference:	TA.5
Course Number:	J-221-2311
Objective:	To train personnel to operate Naval Tactical Command System Afloat (NTCS-A) equipment in support of over-the-horizon targeting (OTHT). Training is accomplished using hardware and software in-stalled in the fleet.
Description:	Consists of classroom presentations and practical laboratory work encompassing the following: OTHT concepts; shore and afloat node functions; communications networks; TPD interoperability; database management functions; battle group OTHT organization/operations.
Audience:	E-4 through E-9.
Clearance:	SECRET
Prerequisites:	Have a minimum of three months operational experience at a NTCS shore or afloat node.
Length:	19 days
Frequency:	24 classes per year
Capacity:	30 students per class
Location:	FCTCLANT Dam Neck, VA
VTC:	NONE
Distance Learning:	NONE
Cost:	Per diem and travel to the training location.
Funding:	By parent organization
Curriculum Manager:	FCTCLANT Dam Neck
CMDSN:	433-7458
CMCOMM:	(757) 433-7458
CMDSNFAX:	433-6613
CMCOMMFAX:	(757) 433-6613
CMCOMME-Mail:	
Scheduling Activity:	OS School Coordinator
SADSN:	227-6755
SACOMM:	(703) 697-6755
SADSNFAX:	223-3544
SACOMMFAX:	(703) 697-3544
SACOMME-Mail:	
Reviewing Activity:	N/A

Title:	**OVER-THE-HORIZON TARGETING/COMMAND, CONTROL, COMMUNICATIONS, COMPUTERS, AND INTELLIGENCE (OTH-T/C4I)**
UJTL Reference:	TA.5
Course Number:	K-2G-0127
Objective:	Provides tactical watch personnel on board TFCC/TWCS/JOTS TDP platforms with an in-depth overview of the OTH/C4I architecture and its operational role in the OTH-T.
Description:	Instruction covers, but is not limited to, OTH-T concepts, weapons, uncertainty, sensors, nodes, basic communications (OTCIXS/TADIXS), database management (BGDBM), ELINT correlation, command and control, and targeting.
Audience:	NTCS-A watch officers and senior officers.
Clearance:	SECRET
Prerequisites:	NONE
Length:	5 days
Frequency:	12 classes per year
Capacity:	16 students
Location:	FCTCPAC, San Diego, CA
VTC:	NONE
Distance Learning:	NONE
Cost:	Per diem and travel to the training location.
Funding:	By parent organization
Curriculum Manager:	FCTCPAC
CMDSN:	553-0852
CMCOMM:	(619) 553-0852
CMDSNFAX:	553-8127
CMCOMMFAX:	(619) 553-8127
CMCOMME-MAIL:	
Scheduling Activity:	FCTCPAC
SADSN:	553-0852
SACOMM:	(619) 553-0852
SADSNFAX:	553-8127
SACOMMFAX:	(619) 553-8127
SACOMME-MAIL:	
Reviewing Activity:	N/A

Title:	**TACTICAL DATA SYSTEMS INTEROPERABILITY**
UJTL Reference:	TA.5
Course Number:	K-2G-0004
Objective:	To give multi-Service officer and senior enlisted personnel experienced in their tactical data system the opportunity to discuss and exchange information necessary to effectively perform data link management and force track coordination functions in a joint environment joint theater of operations.
Description:	Provide a platform for exchange of information and experiences. Format is informal lectures and discussion.
Audience:	E-5 through O-4 data systems managers, operators, and specialists from all armed forces.
Clearance:	SECRET
Prerequisites:	NONE
Length:	2 days
Frequency:	4 classes per year (2 each coast)
Capacity:	40 students per class West Coast; 88 per class East Coast
Location:	FCTCPAC, San Diego, CA
VTC:	Course can be taught on VTC (East Coast only).
Distance Learning:	NONE
Cost:	Per diem and travel to the training location.
Funding:	By parent organization
Curriculum Manager:	FCTPAC
CMDSN:	553-8302
CMCOMM:	(619) 553-8302
CMDSNFAX:	553-8127
CMCOMMFAX:	(619) 553-8127
CMCOMME-MAIL:	
Scheduling Activity:	FCTCPAC
SADSN:	553-8302
SACOMM:	(619) 553-8302
SADSNFAX:	553-8127
SACOMMFAX:	(619) 553-8127
SACOMME-MAIL:	
Reviewing Activity:	N/A

APPENDIX A

JOINT COURSE AND COURSEWARE CATALOG SURVEY

Completion of this survey will assist the USJFCOM Joint Warfighting Center in the further refinement and development of a more comprehensive Joint Course and Courseware Catalog. Please indicate your perceptions of the catalog and provide comments and/or suggested improvements as appropriate. The USJFCOM JWFC will use your input as a basis for updating the catalog.

Please forward to USJFCOM J7/Commander, USJFCOM Joint Warfighting Center, ATTN: Joint Doctrine Division
116 Lakeview Parkway
Suffolk VA 23435-2697

Score each of the following questions.

5	4	3	2	1
EXCELLENT	GOOD	UNDECIDED	FAIR	POOR

____ How useful was the overall format/structure of the catalog?
____ How useful was the table of contents?
____ How useful was the General Information Section?
____ How useful was the Index?
____ How useful was the format for describing course information?
____ How adequate was the depth of information on the courses listed in the catalog?

COMMENTS/SUGGESTED IMPROVEMENTS_____

_____

_____

_____

_____

COMMAND   NAME

TELEPHONE   FAX   E-MAIL   STAFF CODE

COURSE INPUT FORM

Course Title and Number:

UJTL Reference:

Course Objective:

Course Description:

Course Target Audience:

Course Clearance Requirements:

Course Prerequisites:

Course Length:

Course Frequency and Throughput Capacity:

Course Location:

VTC/Distance Learning Capability:

Cost of Attending/Funding Process:

Curriculum Manager/DSN/Commercial Telephone/FAX/E-Mail:

Scheduling Activity/DSN/Commercial Telephone/FAX/E-Mail:

Reviewing Activity/Telephone/FAX:

Please forward to:

> **USJFCOM J7/Commander**
> **USJFCOM Joint Warfighting Center**
> **ATTN: Joint Doctrine Division**
> **116 Lakeview Parkway**
> **Suffolk, VA 23435-2697**

Appendix B

(INTENTIONALLY BLANK)

GLOSSARY OF ACRONYMS

ACC .... Air Combat Command
ADAPT .... Automated Decision making and Program Timeline
ADP .... Automated Data Process(ing)
AETC .... Air Education and Training Command
AFSC .... Armed Forces Staff College
ALMC ....Army Logistics Management College
ALO .... Air Liaison Officer
AOC .... Air Operations Center
ASOC .... Air Support Operations Center
ATO .... Air Tasking Order
ATRRS ....Army Training Requirements and Resourcing System
AUEL .... Automated Unit Equipment List

BCE .... Battlefield Coordination Element

CBW ....Chemical and Biological Warfare
C2W .... Command and Control Warfare
C2WC .... Command and Control Warfare Commander
C4I .... Command, Control, Communications, Computers, and
.... Intelligence
CI ....Counterintelligence
CIA .... Central Intelligence Agency
CINC .... Commander in Chief
CJTF .... Commander Joint Task Force
CNET ....Chief of Naval Education and Training
CPBS .... Capabilities Programming and Budgeting System
CPX .... Command Post Exercise
CRC .... Crisis Reaction Center
CRM .... Collection Requirements Management/Manager
CT.. .... Counterterrorism
CWC ....Composite Warfare Commander

DAISY .... Defense Reutilization Marketing System Computer
.... Support System
DCJTF ....Deputy Commander Joint Task Force
DEA .... Drug Enforcement Agency
DEMIL .... Demilitarization
DIA .... Defense Intelligence Agency
DLA .... Defense Logistics Agency
DOD .... Department of Defense
DODIIS .... Department of Defense Intelligence Information
.... System
DON .... Department of the Navy

153   Appendix C

```
DRMO ............... Defense Reutilization and Marketing Organization
DRMP ....................... Defense Reutilization and Marketing Program
DRMS........................ Defense Reutilization and Marketing System
DSAA ................................ ....... Defense Security Assistance Agency

EEI .................................. ........... Essential Elements of Information
ELINT ...................................... ......................... Electronic Intelligence
EW ...................................... ...................................... ...... Electronic Warfare

FAC ................................... .................................. Forward Air Controller
FBI ................................ ................... Federal Bureau of Investigation
FCTCLANT .......................... Fleet Combat Training Center Atlantic
FCTCPAC .............................. Fleet Combat Training Center Pacific
FID ...................... .............................. Foreign Internal Defense
FITCPAC .......................... Fleet Intelligence Training Center Pacific
FSU .................................. ................................ .. Former Soviet Union
FYDP ........................... ...................... Five Year Defense Program

GDIP ................................ ..... General Defense Intelligence Program
GSR ............................... ........................ Ground Surveillance Radar

HUMINT ................................... ............................ Human Intelligence

I & W ...................................... .............................. Indications and Warning
IDAD ................................. ........... Internal Defense and Development
IDB .................................. ......................................... . Integrated Data Base
IMET ....................... International Military Education and Training
IMINT .............................. ............................... Imagery Intelligence
INS ................................... ........... Immigration Naturalization Service
IRS ...................................... ........................ Internal Revenue Service
IW ...................................... ............................... .... Information Warfare

JCCC ................................. ..... Joint Course and Courseware Catalog
JFACC ............................ Joint Force Air Component Commander
JIC ....................................... ........................ Joint Intelligence Center
JMEMS .............. Joint Munitions Effectiveness Monitoring System
JMIE ................................. ........ Joint Martime Information Element
JMITC .......................... Joint Military Intelligence Training Center
JOPES ................. Joint Operation Planning and Execution System
JPEC ............................. Joint Planning and Execution Community
JPOC ................................... ......... Joint Planning Orientation Course
JSCP ................................ ............ Joint Strategic Capabilities Plan
JSDTC ...................... Joint Strategic Deployment Training Center
JSOFI ............................. Joint Special Operations Forces Institute
JSOTF ............................. ...... Joint Special Operations Task Force
JSPS ................................ ............. Joint Strategic Planning System
```

JSS .... JMIE Support System
JTASC .... Joint Training Analysis and Simulation Center
JTF .... Joint Task Force
JTIDS .... Joint Tactical Information Distribution System
JTS .... Joint Targeting School
JVIDS .... Joint Visually Integrated Display System
JWFC .... Joint Warfighting Center

LAN .... Local Area Network
LPXMED .... Logistics External Processor Medical

MASINT .... Measurement and Signature Intelligence
MDS .... Mission Distribution System
MILFAM .... Military Familiarization
MMSC .... Missile and Munitions School and Center
MOU .... Memorandum of Understanding
MST .... Mobile Support Team
MTT .... Mobile Training Team

NATO .... North Atlantic Treaty Organization
NCO .... Noncommissioned Officer
NDU .... National Defense University
NEO .... Noncombatant Evacuation Operation
NFIP .... National Foreign Intelligence Program
NIC .... National Intelligence Course
NMITC .... Naval Marine Corps Intelligence Training Center
NMJIC .... National Military Joint Intelligence Center
NORAD .... North American Aerospace Defense Command
NSA .... National Security Agency
NTCS-A .... Naval Tactical Command Systems - Afloat
NWC .... Naval War College

OASD-LIC .... Office of the Assistant Secretary of Defense-Low
.... Intensity Conflict
OPLAN .... Operation Plan
OPSEC .... Operations Security
OSD .... Office of the Secretary of Defense
OTC .... Officer in Tactical Command
OTHT .... Over the Horizon Targeting

PADD .... Person Authorized to Direct Disposition
PCS .... Permanent Change of Station
PIF .... Private Index File
POD .... Port of Debarkation
POE .... Port of Embarkation
PPBS .... Planning, Programming, and Budgeting System
PSYOP .... .Psychological Operations

Appendix C

S&TI .... Scientific and Technical Intelligence
SACS .... Southern Association of Colleges and Schools
SAFE .... Support for the Analyst's File Environment
SAP .... Special Access Program
SHAPE .... Supreme Headquarters Allied Powers Europe
SIGINT .... Signals Intelligence
SOF .... Special Operations Forces
SSO .... Special Security Office(r)
STOD .... Special Technical Operations Division

TACP .... Tactical Command Post
TAGS .... Theater Air Ground Systems
TALO .... Theater Airlift Liaison Officer
TDA .... Tactical Decision Aid
TDP .... Tactical Data Processor
TIARA .... Tactical Intelligence and Related Activities
TLAM .... Tomahawk Land Attack Missile
TPFDD .... Time-Phased Force and Deployment Data
TRADOC .... US Army Training and Doctrine Command
TTGLANT .... Tactical Training Group Atlantic

UJTL .... Universal Joint Task List
USAFAGOS .... US Air Force Air Ground Operations School
USCINCPAC .... US Commander in Chief, Pacific
USAFSOS .... US Air Force Special Operations School
USJFCOM .... US Joint Forces Command
USSOCOM ....US Special Operations Command
USSPACECOM .... US Space Command
USSTRATCOM .... US Strategic Command

VGT .... Visual Graphic Transparency
VTC .... Video Teleconference
VTT .... Video Teleconference Terminal

WOC .... Warning Operations Center

Index by Course Title